Forbid(

hypnotic secrets!

Incredible hypnotic confessions of the Rogue Hypnotist!

By the Rogue Hypnotist.

Disclaimer: the Rogue Hypnotist accepts no legal liability for the use or misuse of the information contained in this book. People who are not qualified professionals use the information at their own risk. This book is intended for entertainment and educational purposes only. Only the hypnosis scripts, deepeners etc. contained within are for your personal or public use copyright free. They may not be resold.

Note: British English spelling and American English punctuation is used throughout.

Also available on Amazon in the Rogue Hypnotist series:

'How to hypnotise anyone!' (Amazon.com and Amazon.co.uk no 1 bestseller in hypnosis titles.)

'Mastering hypnotic language!' (Amazon.com and Amazon.co.uk no 2 bestseller in hypnosis titles.)

'Powerful hypnosis!' (Highest rating Amazon.com no 3 and Amazon.co.uk no 2 bestseller in hypnosis titles.)

'Wizards of trance!' (Highest rating Amazon.com no 1 and Amazon.co.uk no 1 bestseller in hypnosis titles.)

CONTENTS

ACKNOWLEDGMENTS

I would like to thank the individual (who shall remain nameless) that pointed out the trance we call 'living.'

Introduction: what they don't want you to know!

Book 1: 'How to hypnotise anyone' –
taught you the simple basic building blocks of
hypnosis.

Book 2: 'Mastering hypnotic language' -
taught you how to use hypnotic language with
more precision.

Book 3: 'Powerful hypnosis' – taught you
how to start using hypnosis for some useful
purpose, what to do and what not to do: it
showed you many methods and techniques
that any hypnotist or therapist can use to
make their work more successful, which I
called 'hypnotic deprogramming.'

If you are a regular.

Before we start on book 4 I would like to
thank anyone that has bought any of my
other books and anyone who has kindly said
nice things about them: I appreciate this
greatly. I hope I have produced something
'juicy' for you in this volume.

If you are new.

My apologies to people who have read my other books but I just have to explain who I am to newcomers; this may be the first book of mine they've purchased.

I am a highly experienced, top Master Practitioner of NLP and clinical hypnosis working reasonably successfully in London, UK. I can rid clients of problems in one, one hour session 99.9% of the time. I have 'cured' people of addictions, depression, OCD, IBS, PTSD you name it; with words alone! I have studied this subject for over 20 years. I have helped TV personalities, millionaires (if you care about this sort of thing, most do unfortunately); primarily I have helped 'ordinary' folk like YOU. In the first few years of practice I had about a 97% success rate, now it is 100%.

Unlike all the losers, second raters, bold morons and freaks who learn hypnosis and NLP to mind control people (yawn) I learnt this stuff to help people. ***The test of a man's character is what he does with any power or influence he may accrue in this***

life.

I decided in late 2013 to give away everything I have learnt; what works, what doesn't in the realm of hypnosis so that your wouldn't waste the time I have – you'd get the central essence of what I know. I know it works because I've actually done it. I teach you in a highly informal and non-academic, non-anemic style. My books are (I hope?!) fun and no NLP/hypnosis is done to you by reading it. **_I want you to think critically about the information I present._**

I am giving this information away for nothing, more or less, because the so-called self-help elite are rip-off artists who charge people huge tons of cash; most are running 'therapy cults.' Most people are so gullible, so naïve about such hucksters that we may safely call them – 'the hard of thinking.' Hypnosis won't make you 'powerful.'

Unlike other twee-minded teachers I go to the places few dare to tread to expose how, shall we say – 'influence' is being used against you. _In fact don't think of me as a 'teacher,' it has too many negative connotations and_ *associations. I am just someone who has acquired useful knowledge from trial and error, and I wish to share the secrets of hypnotic success with **you** for next to nothing, this book is worth 100 live seminars rolled into one. The facts are stripped back to give you the essence of successful hypnotic practice in a B-S free zone.*

With that in mind – on with the show. Of course I still remain anonymous for my own reasons. Success leads to many forms of jealousy.

Now it's book 4: So what are we going to cover???!

Well...this book is primarily about 'waking hypnosis' in all its guises. By the end of it you will be far more knowledgeable about it than most if not all psychologists, shrinks and even 'Master Hypnotists.' Whatever a 'Master hypnotist' is.

I hope this book is a one stop hub for all you really need to know to launch successfully into creating waking hypnosis; the rest you can develop and discover for yourself. It also covers parts of the weird and wacky world of hypnosis that you won't find on the usual hypnosis courses. *It is, in a way a large but interesting footnote to the first 3 books I have written on hypnosis. It will breakdown and drill into you the very specific component parts of most hypnotic phenomena so that you can create your own hypno-tricks, scripts, inductions*...but there's more! After reading this book you will be able to craft your own hypnotic phenomena because you WILL know the underlining principles fully; and when you know that, you're off!!!

- It's a bit of a troubleshooting manual too with a few extra tips on little, often left alone techniques and methodologies that can help hypnotherapist, hypnotist and 'amateur enthusiast' alike. I'll cover some ways hypnotists can use 'symbology' (the use of symbols) to deepen trance and to help people feel good by getting rid of anxiety etc. Also how you can specifically elicit powerful and wonderful emotions using symbols.

- This book will provide detailed analysis
  and proof of the core principles of
  hypnosis stripped of their historical and
  cultural trappings to a crystallised core
  that you can use. Ethically folks!!!! If
  someone's product is good, in time it
  will sell itself others things being equal,
  don't con people using influence
  technologies and then fail to deliver
  what you promised: you just get
  buyer's remorse and a bad reputation.
  **Reputation is everything for the
  small business.**

- We'll also start to cover cults and
  brainwashing in this book: you'll see
  how cults and the techniques of
  brainwashers are actually in use ALL
  around you in wider society. Cults are
  an intense, perverse, destructive
  microcosm of the macrocosm that
  surrounds them.

- You'll learn a very (and amusing)
  potted history of hypnosis; this is
  essential to put the methods in
  historical context: it's also weirdly

interesting, revealing much to the more penetrating mind.

- I'll teach you the very few NLP patterns that are worth knowing in order to help your hypnotherapy clients, with my little Rogue Hypnotist twist thrown in of course.

- I'll teach you multiple pain control techniques including my own 100% successful pain management triple layer treatment for injuries. Hypnosis is THE best pain control technique available to man on this planet: end of story. As a hypnotist, removing, lessening pain is a must.

- I will teach you how to cure 99.9% of phobias and low level anxiety.

- I'll expose 'seductive hypnosis' – how sexual themes and sexual languaging are used in several fields to hypnotise _men and women._ I will show you how to induce any pleasurable feeling state on demand conversationally and otherwise; by doing so we'll briefly analyse how 'sex sells.' **The fact is you've been exposed to sexual hypnosis ALL your life – you just didn't know it – till now.** I'll teach you how certain NLPers and hypnotists use 'sex trances' to make women who don't find them attractive, deeply desire to be their sex toys in very short order. *We'll analyse the hypnotic languaging of international bestseller 50 Shades of Grey's first 2 pages alone to identify why women had no choice but to read it!*

- You'll learn about how the hypnotic power of TV really affects you and yours. Why some songs are hypnotically catchy and how you can use those principles in your communication in general. Make no mistake after reading my books your communication abilities will skyrocket.

- You'll learn about scumbag psychopaths; how to spot one, avoid treating one and about how they have, quite literally, a hypnotically 'spell-binding' power over many *real* humans.

That's right folks a psychopath looks human but it ain't. You'll discover why! You will discover how they hypnotise their victims as a snake does its lunch!

- You'll learn how to better communicate with your own and other's subconscious mind. I'll indirectly teach you how to create hypnosis scripts for self-hypnosis and to help others.

- I'll break down 'ye olde' traditional hypnosis methods and show you how you can modernise them for practical use today: it's really just the same as modern hypnosis but with props! I'll show you how, by just using the imagination, you'll get the same results.

- I'll show you how and why it's better to let people deepen their own trances in unique ways, at least one of which you won't find anywhere else because I invented it.

- This book is an eclectic bag of hypno-tricks that should keep you off the streets for a while my young padawans. Oh you want to know about street hypnosis and surreptitious forms of waking hypnosis (which is going on ALL the time by the way) and all the other goodies as I promised in my last book, 'Powerful hypnosis?' Ok we'll do all that too. *Ready to learn some very interesting and forbidden things? Moo-ha-ha-ha!*

Then let's begin book 4 without further ado...and the best place to begin is at, well, the beginning...

The weird and secret history of hypnosis part 1 – told very quickly.

Hypnosis is weird and its history is weirder! Here are its roots in under a page!

1. **Playing possum:** Many animals have the capacity under stress to enter protective 'trance' states which make them appear dead.

2. **Daydream and focus:** Man is born/created/evolved with a natural capacity to experience trance and hypnosis - what you might call 'trance potential.'

3. **Primitive ritual trance a.k.a 'shamanism':** healers who claim to do so with 'spirit' help facilitated by the trance state. **Methodologies: expectation, authority of shaman/deity, drums, dance, chanting, sensory overload, plausible ritual and suggestion.**

4. **Walk like an Egyptian - 'Civilised' trance:** That we know, Indic civilisation used hypnosis before

anyone else, soon followed over five thousand years ago by the Egyptian Old Kingdom. The Temple of Imhotep in the city of Saqqara becomes a 'healing centre' in late third Century BC through the use of 'temple sleep.'

Methodologies: expectation (suckers would travel for miles to reach site), authority of 'priests'/deity, plausible ritual, eating 'hypnotic' herbs, sensory overload, boredom, repetition through hours of rhythmic chants/ 'prayers,' (which leads to fatigue) sensory deprivation via a 'special darkened chamber.' There the 'patient' awaited a dream which was said to reveal a cure; a.k.a – trusting subconscious wisdom. Dream work very similar to Freud's work too!!! See book 3, 'Powerful hypnosis.'

5. **Greek trance - sleep temples:** Note - the ruling class of ancient (post Homeric age) Greece were of *Egyptian* origin see Herodotus - they brought a

variation of their rites at some point to Greece using 'sleep temples.' They were dedicated to Aesculapius the Greek god of healing. **Methodologies: expectation (of 'divine' intervention no less, a common theme), reassurance of expert knowledge, plausible rituals, sensory overload and direct suggestion to elicit a 'dream cure' in a 'sleep chamber,' these were filled with snakes, the symbol of the God! Think of the symbols of modern medicine which are also snakes! The real snakes would have produced fear/trauma trance or at least a highly focused state: on avoiding being bitten presumably!!! Snakes are symbols of immortality – symbols can cure remember if you've read my other books.** Snakes are used in modern 'revivalist' conversion ritual and traditions to induce fear trance and create sensory overload – a.k.a bombardment!

6. **It's all Greek to me - the Delphi oracle:** Greeks, presumably mainly the wealthy ones, would seek advice from the 'oracle' at Delphi; usually a young girl who through ritual would (a post hypnotic of some kind) enter a 'séance trance' where she would 'become possessed' by the god Apollo and dish out pearls of wisdom which were phrased very much like astrologers' predictions today. Significant political decisions were often based on the 'god's' advice. **Methodologies: expectation, use of 'hypnotic herbs'*, darkened chambers lit with candles and bedecked with 'bright paintings' – sensory deprivation, surreal and narrow focus of attention. The oracle would sit over a 'crack' in the temple through which 'intoxicating vapours' would pour. The hypnotic intent of the oracle would have been a powerful factor in building expectation in both herself and the client.** Interestingly Catholicism and the Byzantine

(Eastern) church use incense in their rituals which they adopted from pagan traditions. (* I will show you in this book how you could do a modern 'hypnotic herb' instant induction using an M and M sweet!!!)

7. **The wilderness years:** with the advent of Christianity ancient formal hypnosis goes into hiding; only to remerge in France in 1774 – two years before the American Revolution, just as the authority of Western Christianity under the rule of the papacy is about to implode!

What ageless hypnotic principles have we unearthed? We have at least 12.

- **The power of expectation:** of the 'client' that 'it will work' and the 'hypnotic intent' of the 'hypnotist.'

- **The power of the authority principle:** this is attained through the perception of secret knowledge or divine/spiritual sanction.

- **The use of plausible ritual:** within a given society's 'belief framework.'

- **The use of 'dumbo's feathers':** also known as 'hypnotic props.'

- **Narrow focus of attention.**

- The use of **'special hypnotic places':** which must be visited to affect cure.

- The use of direct suggestion. (That we know.)

- The use of **repetition.**

- The use of **sensory deprivation.**

- The use of **fatigue.**

- The use of **sensory overload.**

- **The physical induction of trance:** dance, rhythm.

- **Provoking unconscious responses:** dreams, sleep and emotions.

We will discover in this book which ones are absolutely essential to hypnosis and waking hypnosis and ditch the rest. **These ageless hypnotic themes will be systematically repeated and re-discovered throughout the book.**

The history of the hypnotic world part 2 appears later in this book and swiftly covers the history of hypnosis in the modern age up to the 20th century. We will continue with the work of Mesmer. Notice I am using the hypnotic principle of the 'cliff hanger,' your brain wants the 'sense of completion template' to close.

Of secrets, cults and sales.

'Do you want to know a *secret?'*

'*Forbidden* knowledge just a click away!'

'*Taboo* sex secrets revealed!'

'Learn what the masters *really* do!'

'Tired of being *left out* of the loop?'

'Learn what *does* succeed!'

Remember the saying 'curiosity killed the cat?' Well in real life piquing curiosity is the no. 1 way cults, sales people etc. get you hooked. ***Everyone wants to know secrets!*** They are based on the implicit assumption of hidden power. As the saying goes 'knowledge is power.' *If only* I had this secret knowledge I could do x, y, z; you feel like an outsider, these 'secrets' could give me the break I need, right? Maybe. Most of these hypnotic secrets aren't secret at all; it's just hardly anyone can be bothered to do their own research. Everything in my book is known, I've just put my own spin on it; lots of experienced hypnotists know it! Sometimes a lack of knowledge does hold you back: this book will rectify that to some degree I hope, for the aspiring hypnotist or the more advanced ones. Who knows for whom this book could be of use in many interesting and yet unknown ways just when you least expect it?

Creativity: adored, yet despised.

Creativity is a boon and a curse: most people are NOT creative by the time they reach adulthood; it has been knocked out of them by 'the system.' Being creative is like speaking Swahili to an Englishman: he just ain't gonna get it! **Real creativity represents change: a threat to the established order. People don't like it because it raises the prospect of uncertainty.** People are taught early on that creativity is for children, it is 'immature,' incorrect and dangerously so: yet in truth creativity is an essential part of being fully human. Adults like hypnosis because their unfulfilled essential human need for play and imagination is finally fulfilled. Creativity solves all your problems in moments of inspiration, while you sleep, intuitions etc.

Try this with yourself or clients...

- If you have a seemingly unsolvable problem, forget about it. If you wish, imagine you have a note with your problem written on it. Next imagine you put it in a bottle and throw it behind you 'Into your subconscious.' Get on with your life and sooner or later the solution will present itself when you least expect. Relax. The subconscious/unconscious is fully capable of solving problems when you focus on something else. It doesn't need the help of the conscious mind which is far too limited for such a task.

A shockingly funny induction.

When shock occurs people become more suggestible and hypnotisable. Ok, we know this (if you read the first 3 books!); how can we use this principle in a new way? Hold on – what about shockingly funny humour which provides an instantaneous unconscious response?

NOTE TO THE HARD OF THINKING: I try to make my books open to all, idiot proof but with the education system today that is very hard. Just because I put embedded commands in a script doesn't mean you need embedded commands, for my first three years of hypnotherapy practice I used very authoritarian hypnosis and didn't use embeds once! <u>BUT IN MY EXPERIENCE WITH REAL PEOPLE I FOUND HYPNOTHERAPY CLIENTS RESPOND BEST TO A MIXTURE OF DIRECT AND INDIRECT HYPNOSIS.</u>

Guidelines for using embedded commands for newcomers: as you say the embed, lower your tone at the end of the sentence as if giving a command (known as command tonality) and slightly turn your head; this marks out the phrase as being distinct from the surrounding words etc. The subconscious then knows you are talking to <u>it.</u>

Shockingly funny script!

(You can use this as a re-induction, or you can see if it works as a first time one if you want – if they don't seem to 'alter'/drop the head on the trigger, move on to something else: if you act as though it is a fact that this will work with total confidence, you are stacking the odds in your favour. Nothing works 100% of the time, everyone is different!)

'Close your eyes

take a deep breath in for the count of 3...

(Note to hypnotist: you can use this breathing pattern to calm any anxiety – repeat as often as needed)

and release it on a count of 5...

that's it...

and again...

Just start to **get comfy and relax...**

one way that anyone can

go under hypnosis

is to remember nice things...

We all love to laugh don't we?

Laughter is so infectious...

you need to **be very relaxed**

in order to laugh...

as though

a deep down part of you suddenly relaxes

and releases good feelings instantly...

You know when shockingly funny humour is present: **certain states of mind can change instantly when an unexpected trigger is presented...**

(Note to hypnotist: the above line is

used to set up the hypnotic trigger)

Maybe you can remember times when you just couldn't stop laughing?

Some people shriek, howl, boom, blast out with laughter!

Have you ever been surprised by something that made you laugh so much?

Maybe you were in hysterics?

Your eyes watering...

bent over with laughter!

You know **when a surprise occurs you can go into hypnosis fast.**

All you need to do is remember a time when you laughed at something that shocked you in a wonderfully pleasant way...

We've all had that experience...

Remember it vividly...

What you saw...

Heard...

Felt...

DEEP SLEEP! *(Option: clap your hands hard!)*

(I **distract that conscious mind** with the memory and then having that state – hit it fast with an unexpected hypnotic command.)

Advertising works!

I just went to Toys R Us to buy Christmas presents. As we walked around the store they now and again played adverts for Toys R Us; I thought, that's a bit much, we're already in the shop! Anyway, wandered around not thinking anymore of it, got some lovely toys after an hour's hunting. When driving home, a lady who accompanied me on my trip said,

'Toys R Us is really good value – it's got everything you need under one roof...'

She said it in a robotic, trancey kind of way. I replied,

'That's the slogan from their adverts! They've brainwashed you!'

Rather embarrassed she realised it was. She watches tons of TV too! And adverts don't work – riiiiight!

A relaxing hypnotic re-induction.

The next induction I'll give you is a re-induction process I used with a man who came to see me over a period of three years. Its purpose was to induce deep physical and mental relaxation, which trust me, he needed. With multiple visit clients I will invent tailor-made induction scripts just for them.

Relaxing re-induction script.

'Just close your eyes as usual...

That's it, just shuffle and get comfy

as you prepare again

to go into trance...

Again, just focus on your breathing...

draw all of your attention to

your breathing

that's it...

you know the way...

you've done this many times

in fact you're an expert

about **going into deep hypnosis...**

Once again can you take in a deep breath for me...

and just hold it...

and just slowly let it out...

Perfect...

Just vividly recall the last time

you were **entering a state of wonderful hypnotic trance, now...**

Can you recall just how wonderful it felt

in mind and body...

as if **it's happening now!**

DEEP SLEEP!　　(Re-induction trigger...watch for an immediate change.)

100 times deeper than last time　　(or whatever figure was agreed)

just like that...

Each out breath relaxes you even more, does it not?

Notice perhaps feelings,

images, pleasant fantasies...

sensations that captivate you

inside now...

because feelings,

images and sounds,

music perhaps

can and will **deepen this state...**

Allow all the muscles of your head to **relax right now,**

around your eyes especially...

to **become calm,**

soft,

loose,

limp and very relaxed...

very deliciously lazy...

feel how good that feels

as all of those muscles

let go of that tension, now...

that pressure they'd been holding onto

unnecessarily...

Feel that relaxation spread

down your neck now (relaxing people head downward seems best – also suggestive of 'going down' into hypnosis)

allowing all the muscles,

all the nerves,

and all the fibres in your neck to

relax deeply now...

feeling smoothed out...

softer,

looser,

limp

and very, very heavy...

There is **no pressure here,**

just peace...

No need to try in vain to be perfect here...

just accepting...

of so many things..

whatever happens

you can utilise it...

no longer fighting...

how can you use whatever happens to your advantage? (Multi-level therapeutic reframe.)

Thinking flexibly,

letting go *of that old black and white thinking* ('black and white' thinking is associated with stress)

now...

Feel how good that feels...

allow that relaxation to spread

down to your shoulders

and back,

loosening every muscle,

feeling oh so wonderful, now...

and

going all the way down *the* **rest** *of
your body...*

as you simply

become utterly absorbed *by the
process of deep relaxation...*

any remaining tension eventually relaxes...

Your brain can relax

and enjoy this peaceful feeling too.

*All tension in your mind just drains out of
you...*

and you **go deeper,**

further enthralled by becoming

further relaxed...

The sound of the clicking clock takes you deeper...

The sound of anything at all...

cars outside just take you deeper...

*just takes you deeper, deeper **still***

and does not bother you in any way

as you simply

ignore distractions.

And the golden rule of deep hypnosis is –

the deeper you go, the better you feel

and the better you feel the deeper

you can go, now...

Just let it be as if

someone kind

has pulled a wave

of blissful relaxation over you

and you just **go deeper**

as a result...

Just **let go even more**

with every exhalation...

Your subconscious mind is your friend

it cares about you very deeply...

and it can

send a wave,

multiple waves

of profound relaxation

from your head to your toes, now (allow time for this to happen)

and **go deeper...**

You may find that you can **go deeper still**

as I'm quiet for a few seconds... (pause.)

Good!

You are doing very well

(always be encouraging, most people don't receive enough of the encouragement they deserve)

Let every exhale

be as if

you are going down *a path of exhalations...*

and each one takes you deeper...

Let it be as if someone has pulled the plug

on that old level of mind-body **tension...**

and it **drains right out** *of you, now.*

As **your body relaxes your mind relaxes so deeply...**

Your entire self, relaxes and

you **go deeper** *and* **become more peaceful, inside...**

The peace of **deep calm** *in all your muscles...*

every fibre and cell

of that body **relaxing deeply...**

You have reached a lovely level of relaxation,

have you not?

Head and body relaxed.

Brain and mind relaxed.

Imagine **your brain is becoming soothed, calm,**

so peaceful...

so much so that perhaps

you can daydream...

and as the deeper you listens

as the other has no need to now...

your mind is now very receptive

to any good ideas...

Any remaining tension eventually relaxes...

as we **focus on other things**

your soothed brain can **relax infinitely deeper**

as you

allow deep unconscious, hypnotic processes to take over...

so that all residual tension

drains right out of your mind...

and you **go deeper,**

further and further relaxed.

You'll keep a deeper level of

over-all relaxation *after this session,*

it will remain with you, **now...**

As you take your next hypnotic breath

and as you let that breath go...

just **go deeper** *and deeper*

than ever before

a place where my words become your

thoughts,

your thoughts become your unconscious beliefs...

a state of pure

mental and physical calm, now

Take that feeling you feel

and **go even deeper...**

that blissful feeling intensifies,

sweeping beautifully

from the top of your head

to the tips of your toes...

from the soles of your feet

to the palms of your hands...

with every hypnotic breath   (there is a hypnotic rate of breathing; breathing and emotional states will be discussed in this book; aren't you lucky!)

growing more limp,

loose,

more **deeply relaxed...**

<u>*Permissive eye catalepsy module.*</u>

Now I would like you

to relax those tiny muscles in your eyelids,

like an nice, warm damp flannel/cloth has been placed over them...

maybe you remember doing that as a child (pleasant age regression)

relax all those muscles completely;

so loose, so profoundly relaxed,

so deliciously

languidly

lazy...

that you want to **totally relax them**

You know you don't have to open them for a while...

you could (this permissive 'could' gets rid of

'resistance')

but you don't want to

it just feels too good this way...

give that area a rest for a while...

and just let your blissful feelings of comfort

take you deeper and deeper

to precisely where you need to go

to get what you want today...

Emotional state deepener.

In a second I'm going to ask you

to **remember something very funny**

that happened to you...

and then I want you to go 10 times deeper...

now, go ahead and remember that hilarious time...

(Pause for a few seconds to allow processing but not too long, the memory serves as the 'deepener trigger' mainly – see book 2,

'Mastering hypnotic language.')

Ten times de-eper,

that's right!

In a second

I'm going to ask you to

remember a time when you were blissfully happy...

and then go twice as hypnotically relaxed

as you are right now...

Go ahead

and remember that blissfully happy time...

that's it.

Lovely...

You can interrupt those old, unhelpful patterns easily –

two times more entranced...

Now double that relaxation

in your own way

because as I said

you are an expert in going into deep hypnosis and trance... (this creates, through verbal reward, a strong 'talent' for hypnosis in future)

it's so wonderfully easy for you to do so...

Now, just allow your mind to

remember a time when you were

oh so deliciously relaxed...

and as you do

your body follows your mind

to re-experience

that wonderful kind of relaxation now.

It may have been on a beach on holiday/vacation

or a day out...

a time when you

get away from it all for a while,

or after working in the yard/garden

or after a workout

or a sports activity...

a time when you were so relaxed

as if you could **relax all the way down**

to your bones...

You are floating into a blissful

hypnotic oblivion, now...

like a feather you've seen on the wind...

or a leaf in autumn perhaps?

Floating down (some clients feel kind of 'floaty' when hypnotised)

down...

do-wn... (your voice should be getting deeper and slower as indicated by book 1, 'How to hypnotise anyone.')

That's right.

Hypnotic dial installation.

What if you have an 'hypnotic dial'...

that actually determines the depth

of the deep hypnotic trance

that you can achieve?

Imagine that and just adjust it accordingly in your mind...

anything that I say

or you think

or imagine,

anything that you feel,

anything you experience

will guide you more intensely deeper... (all experience is linked to going deeper)

You can

enter a more profound state of hypnosis,

a more responsive state of hypnosis...

whenever you wish...

each breath effortlessly eliminates residuals of any kind...

drifting in comfort...

a more comfortable feeling...

letting yourself be pulled

far deeper than ever, inside now...

relax

even further...

<u>*Word trigger - triple level deepener.*</u>

In a moment I will say a word imbued with deep hypnotic power,

I will say that word three times,

each time I say it you'll go even deeper still,

and when those wonderful hypnotic feelings only intensify...

you'll only want to go deeper still

because it feels good to feel that good

And when I say that word the third time

that's your cue

each and both of you

to go through the floor...

plunge willingly into a perfect state of deep hypnotic sleep,

that feels absolutely amazing and wholly fantastic!

Ok – are you ready?

Get set...

and

POMEGRANITE! (Why not? They'll never expect it! The 'hypnotic' word is irrelevant.)

(Pause)

POMEGRANITE!

(Pause)

POMEGRANITE!'

(Do whatever change work you desire now.)

Why are some songs so damned catchy!??

Be careful what music you listen to. The physical indications of listening to a catchy song are? Repeating it over and over and over in our heads and (gasp) tapping a foot! ***Music affects behaviour – end of story.*** Why are some songs *so* catchy? Technically such songs are known as 'earworms,' coined by a James Kellaris a marketing professor at the University of Cincinnati.

Earworms seem to have catchy rhythms, choruses and chord progressions.

So how do they make an earworm so infectious?

If you could perfect this technique, you might become rich beyond your wildest dreams. Jingles are designed to **infiltrate your memory** for years, popping up from *out of nowhere* (the unconscious). There are lots of theories as to what factors produce 'catchiness.' Listen to the languaging – it's that of infection, disease. I have selected a few below.

Chord progressions: according to some researchers especially - I, IV, V, I and I, V, VI, IV. I have no idea what these Roman numerals mean; if you are musical they may make sense!

Repetition: Hypnotic! 'You spin me right round baby right round, like a record baby right round, right round etc.'

Synthesisers: 'Robotic' is best! Hypnosis recordings usually use this artificial approach as opposed to real instruments. Think of all those catchy 80s hits!

These songs hijack our brain in the following way!

It's 1974, flares are in: Baddely and Hitch claim to discover what they called the 'phonological loop.' This being?

The phonological store - the 'inner ear,' which remembers sounds in chronological order.

The articulatory rehearsal system - your 'inner voice,' which repeats these sounds in order to enable easy recall.

Note: This part of the brain is essential in early childhood for developing vocabulary and in adulthood for learning new languages. Catchy songs hijack this auditory 'slave system' of our inner ear, much like the visual 'slave system' of our mind's eye!!!

Some white-coated boffins have claimed catchiness is improved by...

Short and simple melodies: are more likely to get stuck in your head. 'A-ha, a-ha! Staying alive, staying alive etc.'

Interestingly, earworms affect non musicians worst and 'bother' women more than men. OCD sufferers are often tormented by them.

'Musicologist' (what the hell is that??!) Dr. Alison Pawley and psychologist Dr. Daniel Mullensiefen from the University of London claim catchiness is created by:

Longer and detailed 'musical phrases': The ***breath*** a singer takes as they sing a line is vital to sing-along-ability. The longer a vocal/lyric is in one breath, the more likely we are to copy.

Higher number of pitches in the chorus hook: The more _**variety of sounds**_ there are the more infectious. A combination of 'longer musical phrases and a hook over three different pitches,' was best.

Men's voices: Singing along to a song may be _**a subconscious war cry mimic,**_ tapping into our innate tribal wiring. Men lead battles so we are more likely to follow.

'Higher' male voices with noticeable 'vocal effort': High energy, purpose, plus a _**narrower**_ vocal range. (Think the Bee Gees etc.)

Other factors include:

Songs that are _**questions**_ - drives the listener's curiosity! It opens a loop which seeks completion.

The topic of the song must be _**crystal clear**_ to the listener. So simplicity is essential.

**Paints a verbal picture** or _**suggests an image**_ in the mind of the listener.

Unique titles that bring to mind a _**clear image.**_

Catchy song themes and titles often include:

Colour, **place**, a **specific time**, a specific **woman's/girl's name**, contain the word '**night**' (sexual imagery) or '**if**' (activates imagination) use **folk language**/everyday sayings, elicit **powerful emotional states** i.e. breaking up, love, sex, romance etc., state **direct commands** (Beat it!), use **alliteration**, **simile** and **metaphor**, **express fantasies** such as the need to escape a situation (emotional needs not met), use **arresting visual images**, use **antonym**, (*Everybody's Got the Right to be Wrong, If I Could Just Remember to Forget, The High Cost of Low Living, My Future Just Passed* – this is the 'apposition of opposites' to be covered later), use **word play**, known **film or book titles** (re-association) use **personification** (isomorphism) - attributing human characteristics to inanimate objects; *in hypnosis we use ALL of this!*

Hypnosis is truly lurking everywhere. You can learn how to be more hypnotic from so many sources! If you take the time to study. I am reminded of Orwell's 'versificator' in 1984, a machine which produces sentimental musical pap for the proles. As a 19th century opera singer once said, 'Sing 'em muck, it's all they want!'

How to reframe EVERY problem.

When treating 'mental health problems' of any kind it may behove the reader to bear the following principle in mind; I have touched on this in my third book but have found a more succinct expression of it now:

'Every response to a challenge (no matter how maladaptive) is a genuine attempt to overcome that challenge.'

What's the difference between hypnosis and propaganda?

Simple:

Hypnosis, especially of the therapeutic variety produces profound hypnotic **calm, a peaceful, relaxing state of mind** and body through the medium of suggestion.

Propaganda uses the principles of hypnosis to **create a highly emotional state in the subject/receiver:** when you are emotionally aroused through suggestion you become more 'stupid,' less rational, more hysterical, more easily led. You are more likely to take the suggested steps (i.e. desired action) for remedying that emotional arousal by the propagandist. I will cover mass hypnosis thoroughly in book 5: 'Wizards of trance!'

A covert convincer and compliance test.

I don't like 'compliance tests' (is someone following hypnotic instructions) and I don't like fractionation (hypnotising, waking someone up quickly and then sending them back under etc. on and on) even though it works. But you can use both to do a covert compliance test IF you want to build more complex convincers and hypnotic phenomena – arm lifts, hallucinations etc. Do the following...

- Hypnotise subject.

- After a few deepeners...

- Fractionate thus...

'In a few seconds I'll simply say 'open'

when I do you can open your eyes feeling great...

and as soon as I say 'close' your eyes will close

*and you'll **go deeper and deeper into hypnosis feeling wonderful.***

Each time I say (don't say 'tell' you're being sneaky) *'close'*

after I've said 'open' (a bit confusing)

you can go deeper and deeper each time.

Ok? Easy isn't it?

Ready?'

(As you give the exduction command 'open' and they open their eyes you have 'hypnotic compliance,' each time you say the re-induction command 'close' – and they close their eyes you have 'hypnotic compliance' – geddit!? To the hypnotee it's just you saying 'open,' 'close,' 'open,' 'close' etc. (who resists that?!) but IF they do as you suggest they are displaying compliance no matter what *they* think. When you have them following a *seemingly simple instruction* you can then do eye closure tests, hand stick tests etc. You start simple and build. It's just an option for you. Try it out.)

What's a thought virus and why you should care.

There are lots of differing explanations as to what a thought virus is. Most are stupid. ***This is mine: any stupid and thoughtless idea that other people act upon without knowing why.*** Fashion is a great example of a thought virus. Let's take that girl who can't act from the Harry Potter movies: she got a new haircut about a year ago, a very short, kind of boyish, hermaphroditic look. Within a week I saw several girls with that haircut. When David Beckham the world famous football (soccer) player from England used to grow a beard, goatee, get a tattoo, change his hairstyle - young teenage boys and some younger still would copy it (the youngest did not get the beard and tats!). *Really a thought virus is a 'mindless copying virus.'* If it was a 'thought' virus it could just stay in someone's head and not bother the rest of us. Essentially this is a visual cue post hypnotic command.

The night of the living Santas!

One of the most stupid thought viruses is when lots of mindless yuppies in London gather around Trafalgar square and congregate in the pubs thereabouts dressed as Santa/Father Christmas! They take on a herd identity and instead of spreading goodwill and cheer come late December they start fights and drink too much; they become aggressively territorial and develop an antagonism to non 'Santa clones'!!! I am 100% telling you the truth; I witnessed this one December. Some loser arranges it on the Internet every year. It's like a one evening cult of violent Santas! 'Zombies eat brains!' This is waking hypnosis folks. Too much free time...

A good example of a thought virus is a 'craze': yo-yos, hula hoops etc.

Waking hypnosis weapon 1: your hypnotic stare variant 1,2,3 etc.

You can get waking hypnosis alone by getting someone to stare at something: a fireplace, a candle (natural waking hypnosis), a beautiful naked woman if it's a man, a pile of cash if it's a woman. Just joking ladies. Now all that aside, let's start with your stare! That's right any hypnotist worth their weight in gold needs a damn good hypno-glare! You've seen it in the movies with the Svengali hypno-creep and here's the thing - it works. Psychopaths use it too, as you will learn later.

How do you practise this? There are many ways and approaches. You can...

- Draw some eyes on paper or use photoshop etc. and practise looking at the two fake eyes you created: staring into them. Some suggest a black sheet with two red circles/eyes (I find this a bit evil but it's your choice!): it might make you too intense.

- You can also try this: practise keeping your eyes open for just 60 seconds without blinking. That's it; it's actually quite easy.

- Psychopaths aside most reasonably confident people usually hold eye-contact in bursts of 6-7 seconds, looking in a triangle from eye to eye to mouth. That's a generalisation but that is the usual unconscious pattern, or so the researchers tell us. *When you look calmly into someone's eyes for just slightly longer than usual (there is NO need to be intense), they will become slightly uncomfortable: it is a pattern interrupt.* Notice newsreaders and actors blink little on screen: it makes you look 'weak,' low status. Politicians too have been trained to do this: watch them in interviews, rarely do they avert their eyes from the interviewer or blink. It's completely abnormal but because you are used to seeing it on TV you think it is; that's why untrained members of the public can seem to look 'amateurish' or perhaps uncomfortable on the goggle box. They are not, they are behaving normally. Anyway back on point: when you look into your hypnotee's eyes they will avert them. Blink quickly then if you must and then carry on as before.

- As you continue your hypno-gaze (a gaze is better than staring which is intimidating or suggestive of sexual interest) two things will probably happen. They will let out a sigh or their eyes will glaze and trance out. That's the sign you got 'em! They are in light waking hypnosis at this point. But look out for other trance indicators: stillness, facial flushing etc., see book 1 for more details on signs of trance.

- You can then IMMEDIATELY start giving suggestions. Easy-peasy. You can do it with confidence. *Your specific hypnotic actions will lead to hypnotic reactions.*

- In my sessions with clients I do not use full on hypno-glares; the English do not like being stared at, it makes them uncomfortable and aggressive. Now and again and very subtly I will make full eye contact and hold it a bit longer than usual, not too long, not creepy just a nice relaxed eye gaze.

- If a man stares at a woman close up as though 'intensely evaluating' her she may well jump back as though stunned or hit. She can feel the intensity of the look.

- People can tell if they are being stared at even if they cannot see the person who is staring! Do this experiment if you have net curtains, which are going out of fashion but they are wonderful because I can look at passers-by and clients and I can see how they are reacting/behaving when they think they are unobserved, this is a great way to get a sense of true character, feeling and mood. Anyway, net curtains completely veil you to the conscious mind. *BUT in some individuals the subconscious detection mechanisms are so very powerful that they can detect the 'force' of being* _watched!_ The person looks up or at the curtains or at the house as if they know they are under 'surveillance': it is amazing but only some men, women and children can detect it. Bizarre!!! Is this some half-hidden ability to protect us from attack? It must be the origin of the saying 'eyes in the back of your head.' It truly is an unexplained '6th sense' of Man.

- Look into someone's eyes till their 'reality orientation' gets fidgety – they might look nervous or slightly fearful.

- Look into someone's eyes until the eyes/face express that they expect _'something to happen.'_

- Say, 'I'm a MASTER HYPNOTIST!' Then stare at them 'priming' the subconscious that some total weirdness is on the verge of happening. Look at them until the pupils get bigger or a 'look of readiness' occurs. This look is explained later.

- You can get fake eyes and get people to look into them and say – *'As you look at them you get more and more tired, your eyes feel heavy, more and more sleepy* (pretend to yawn!) – *you just want to close those eyes...etc.'* Seriously!

My first mini-waking trance.

I was flat broke and she was my first client; I'd only hypnotised my mum, one of her best friends and my best friend to give him the b***s to be able to talk to girls. Now I had a real client and a chance to earn £80s!!! Just for stopping someone smoke. I (for some clueless reason) agreed to go around this woman's house. I was very nervous but did my best to hide it. I got her under quickly doing something like the following, to my great relief; she was actually hyper-responsive! I have added embeds to improve it, originally there were none.

Stare at anything induction.

'It's now time to **relax deeply...**

Just stare at some point on the wall...

Really notice all the details of it...

The way the light hits it...

Take a deep breath and relax on that out breath...

Just **focus on your breathing...**

(splitting consciousness/overload)

as you stare at that point...

you may hear different sounds...

the sound of my voice...

thoughts, images might pass through your mind... (describing experience)

continue **feeling peaceful...**

Quieter...

remain comfortable...

You can **concentrate** *on the importance of what I say....*

as it allows you to **relax a little more...**

Let go of tensions *and just*

enjoy being relaxed *as you*

stare at that point...

As you continue breathing...

you can hear my voice...

sometimes it's audible...

sometimes not...

it might sound far away... (covering all options)

but you can't turn your ears off

or your eyes off

but

*you can **close your eyelids over them...***

She closed her eyes! Yippee! I couldn't believe it worked! I had no idea that I had induced waking trance though, right up till the point when I suggested she close her eyes. 'Mazing. I'll teach you more advanced stuff as we progress.

Finding somnambulists amongst the maddening crowd.

The best subjects, the **hyper-responsive** ones are always the most fun to work with; they tend to be playful, easy to talk to, talkative, engaging, imaginative, charming and funny. Traits to look for are:

1. When talking to a group of people about hypnosis look for the one that shows 'response potential' – this is the one that has gone pop-eyed/glassy-eyed just at the mention of hypnosis.

2. People who talk in their sleep or sleep walk.

3. Did they have an imaginary friend as a child?

4. Did they enjoy imaginative play on their own?

5. Did they have parents who encouraged imaginative play? (If they had parents who said at age 1 and a half – 'Jimmy, it's time you grow up and start thinking about your

future in accountancy...' they may not be so ripe, yet!)

6. People who are interested in or have undergone handwriting analysis.

7. People who are interested in the 'New Age' – complete and utter somnambulists! They are in a semi-permanent waking trance. I call them 'space cadets.'

8. Anyone who has 'successfully' used a Ouija board; I won't touch those things with a barge pole! 99% of the time a Ouija board is just ideomotor signalling from the creative subconscious. It's the 1% that concerns me!

9. They have been successfully hypnotised before. You can trance hijack and revivify the old hypnotic trance state quickly. They also know what to expect.

10. Look for people with sparkly eyes, that is those bright pin-pricks/highlights that twinkle: it means they have good imaginations, these are the ones with life zest in them! Avoid the dead-eyed ones.

11. Anyone who regularly goes to see a psychic or fortune teller.

12. Very creative people are the best of all! Actors are in waking trance when performing (at least the good ones are!), film students, young people studying fine art at college etc. Architects make good subjects as they are constantly visualising possibilities of what could be professionally.

13. Someone who is bubbling over with total enthusiasm and curiosity to learn about hypnosis or experience it directly but hasn't yet. You can create this excited anticipation state which is THE perfect priming state for hypnosis and especially 'instantaneous' hypnosis by talking up your abilities etc.!

14. Hypnosis junkies – those who love the stoned, 'out of it' feeling of trance. They'll volunteer first and then again and again and again. I think they should be called hypno-bitches because I've quite seen a few and they love being owned. Weird.

15. Those who are in a group situation which de-individuates a person and makes them suggestible. This is an ancient survival mechanism that exists to make humans in groups (especially Northern Europeans) suggestible in order to promote group cohesion to fight off large prey animals. At the biological level humans are a cursorial* pack species. *Cursorial means predators that wear down a prey using 'endurance' methods.

16. Those who have witnessed someone else being successfully hypnotised. Monkey see, monkey do.

17. Those who can pretend to be hypnotised. Explained in appendix.

18. Those who have heard of a particular hypnotist's prestige one way or another.

19. Palm reading, tarot card junkies etc.

20. A soldier etc. Think about it, they volunteer to be ordered about!

I will show you a somnambulist test later on.

Accountants are the lame ducks of hypnosis in my experience. They can go into hypnosis alright but they take training to go really deep: the job and those like it devoid of imaginative capacity are just not one that encourages a playful mindset; to say the least! I am reminded of the Monty Python sketch where the accountant says he wants to be a lion tamer!

The idiot proof guide to 'instantaneous inductions' level 1.

'When I do x you will fall into an instantaneous hypnotic sleep!'

That is THE formula my Padawan; it IS that simple. Structurally this is all most stage hypnotist do. Remember they are looking for the **hyper-responsive** hypnotees. But first the person must be primed and in the 'hypnotic mood.' If they are, just choose a trigger for the subconscious to take as its cue for instantaneous hypnosis! *I'll give you some examples but it doesn't matter what you do as long as the person is ready.* They must be in the state a runner is before he hears, 'On your marks, get set, GO!'

I say give a three stage repetitive cue/trigger to prime the subconscious. Look, the subconscious knows it can trigger hypnosis it just needs a plausible ritual. I am adding in eye fixation to improve concentration and load things in your favour but it's not needed if someone is primed and eager AND A SOMNAMBULIST! If so rub hands in glee and play with them!

Finding somnambulist test.

4 options follow...

'Look at this pen. Focus on it totally. In a moment I will tap my pen on this desk 3 times. On the third tap you will immediately fall into a deep hypnotic sleep!'

'Very soon I will ask you to gaze at that spot on the wall...as you do I will say the word SLEEP 3 times. On the third utterance of the word sleep you will fall instantaneously into deep hypnosis and it will feel wonderful!'

'Look at one of your fingernails intently. When I click my fingers 3 times your eyes will close and you will fall automatically into the most profound state of deep hypnotic sleep that you possibly could!'

A last one for someone you know is a great subject is...

'Look into my eyes. In only a few seconds time I will shoot you with the hypno-gun (use a banana or your hand) and when I do you will instantly fall into deep hypnosis! 1-2-3 BANG!'

The formula is...

1. Focus.

2. In a moment x will happen.

3. Fire trigger.

You can use this in stage shows or for therapy clients IF they'd like it. You could set it up through rewording as a re-induction trigger, knock your socks off!

But here is the way to do it solely linguistically:

Instantaneous linguistic induction.

'Close your eyes

and **focus on your breathing...**

that's it...

just **focus on it completely...** (Focus of attention.)

Soon – I'll do something that is powerfully hypnotic...

it will allow you to **enter hypnosis instantly on my cue...**

I won't say as you **relax deeply and rest**

what that cue will be...

but your subconscious will instantly recognise it and let you

fall instantly into deep hypnosis on my cue... (Priming for hypnosis.)

Ok...

Ready?

Just for yourself **in your own mind...**

I don't need to know it because

you already know it

and it's a secret

it's private,

none of my business...

So just **remember...**

*the name of your best friend when you were 5
and see them in your mind's eye!*

Deep sleep!' (Command them with
forceful purpose and intent, but don't shout.)

This sort of stuff works about 97% of the
time: I actually only save it for my most
hyper-responsive clients because they all
expect and deserve the results they paid for;
in other words I do what works. Their head
may well drop or they just go still. If you
suspect that trauma may be linked to
remembering the above then ask them what
birthday/Christmas presents they got age 6,
what their favourite teacher's name was at
school, what was the number of their first
house, what year did they go to school, how
old or what year they passed their driving test
etc., get the idea? *You set up the cue –
occupy consciousness with a memory retrieval
task and then say the command trigger.* With
good subjects it will work. I remember doing
something like this with a highly sceptical
older gentlemen. He smiled as I set up the
cue as if to say 'that won't work on me' – out
like a light! Head dropped, the whole

caboodle! If it don't work move on. Plenty more tricks to get 'em with.

In my next book: 'Wizards of trance!' I will show you how to use your hands and touch (non-verbal) to induce trance.

Why you should always be confident when hypnotising folks.

Look the reality is *hypnosis works.* People love to be hypnotised; just relax and follow the recipes I've given you and success is assured when you add a dash of common sense and adaptation to personality and circumstance. **Please make this stuff your own: whenever I took a hypnosis/NLP course I would immediately rewrite what I was taught, always.** Have a let's see what happens attitude: do focus on outcome but remember one strategy is just that; mentally fixating or hoping to God the one thing you learnt will work will make you tense. Often just KNOWING it will work helps. *The things I teach you inevitably elicit hypnotic responses.* You can say to people before hypnotising them...

'Would you like to do something hypnotic?'

'Let's play around with this...etc.'

Think playful and fun and you'll relax and so will they. Remember your mood will infect the subject.

Hypno-dog! My first exposure to live stage hypnosis.

The first live stage hypnosis show I ever saw and the last was with a man who had a dog that 'hypnotised' people. I was interested in NLP and hypnosis even before I went to University to study film making. It was a night out for everyone who lived in the student house we all shared. We had overdressed because we didn't get out much. Anyway, the hypnotist, a very affable, professional man in his late forties I guess came out and asked for volunteers. All the show offs and egotists and exhibitionists got up. The hypnotist had a lovely black Labrador – he was the star. I remember the hypnotist got the volunteers to stare at the Fresnel stage lights to induce trance.

The highlight of the show was when the black dog starred at people and they went into hypnosis. This had been set up as,

'When the hypno-dog stares at you you'll instantly go into hypnosis!'

This dog had been trained to stare

hypnotically at people – it was weirdly funny and it worked. _True 'instant' (I mean they drop in one second with no set up) hypnosis occurs ONLY in highly primed somnambulists and by setting up ANY re-induction trigger._ Anything can be given as a cue for hypnosis to re-occur. Seeing doors knobs – whatever.

I have been trained by the best authoritarian hypnotist in the world and he could get people under quick first time but _instantly?_ I never saw that happen.

Mumnosis.

(UK mum = US mom)

Covered in my earlier books:

'Mummy kiss it better,'

...and it is better: waking hypnosis. Mums control children's behaviour by saying,

'I've got eyes in the back of my head you know.'

Installing the fear of consequences from naughty behaviour!!! This can be termed 'mumnipotence.' Look out for examples of mumnosis, they are all around you.

Waking hypnosis in dentistry and medicine.

Waking hypnosis is achieved without any seemingly formal induction. It uses all the same principles as 'eyes closed' hypnosis. *99.9% of people are potentially suggestible ALL THE TIME!* They are especially so when they are unwell and in need of medical help. Doctors and nurses have been using waking hypnosis for ages! Some don't even know they're doing it.

1. A man visits a nurse. She is to use a piece of high tech equipment on him. She carries out the treatment and he says he feels much better. After he leaves she notices she didn't plug it in.

2. A man visits a dentist. The dentist tells his patient that he will need to use a pain killer (*pain KILLER!* The languaging!!) for some work that must be performed. He dips a cotton ball into the pain killer. He carries out the dental work; the patient experiences no pain during the procedure. In reality the dentist had deliberately dipped the cotton ball in water.

3. A doctor treats a man requiring a gas mask which emits 'pain control medicine.' Man puts on mask and breathes deeply. Medical procedure is carried out with patient experiencing no pain. There was absolutely no gas that passed through the mask.

4. Late 19th century. Woman visits doctor for facial pain. She truly believes hypnosis will help. He places her hand on her face over the painful area and suggests that the pain is going away and that she feels better. In quick order she does.

Let's break these down and analyse them.

1. What happened in case one? Both patient and nurse **expect** that said machine is plugged in; both act honestly **as if** it is. Man is healed. In other words the man **expected** a **plausible healing ritual** would heal him, his subconscious did the rest.

2. In the second case the patient **expected** a 'pain killer' to be used. The dentist acted **as if** there was one. A **plausible healing ritual** is performed.

3. Case three? As above...Mask **fixates**

attention on face AND he is told to **breathe deeply.**

4. Finally: woman **expects** (an almost secular religious belief) hypnosis WILL work. She is primed and **anticipates** success before seeing a doctor. Doctor acts as though what she said is true – he reinforces her **expectation.** He places her hand on her painful face – **fixation of attention.** Simple suggestions of gradual pain relief given. I include a modernised version of this full procedure below.

Ok – so what did we learn needs to occur for waking hypnosis?

- The **authority figure MUST be confident in the successful outcome.**

- The **subject must have a good expectation that the 'procedure' will work.**

- A **plausible ritual must occur.** This somehow marshals unconscious healing mechanisms.

- **Fixation of attention on something** – a cotton ball, a mask, breathing, a hand, a device. Also note *physical sensations focused upon.* See book 1, 'How to hypnotise anyone.'

- In case three the man is also told to breathe deeply which will **relax** him.

Can we conclude: essentials for waking hypnosis?

In order of procedural importance.

An authority figure.

A subject/hypnotee.

A two way confident expectation of success.

A plausible ritual.

Fixation of attention on some physical process of any kind.

What's the *real* difference between this and

other types of hypnosis? Zero! The lesson? Note - hospitals, hospices and nursing homes initiate hypnoidal trance states in patients. When people are undergoing surgery or are in a coma they are programmable – be careful what you say to them: be positive.

The human mind accepts what it is primed to EXPECT - even if that anticipated thing does not occur in reality – it acts as though it did! BONKERS!!! A good example is a startle response when being told a ghost story.

My version of pain removal waking hypnosis.

(1. Take one of subject's hands and hold it. 2. Place their free hand on the painful area.)

'Close your eyes please. (Not needed but why not? Sensory focus facilitated.)

As I hold your hand

and as you hold your other one on that painful part (consciousness is split between both hands causing overload) *you immediately* **start to feel relief...** (I have included embeds but it can be done without them)

*Soon, very soon...***the feeling of relief grows...** (Soon - 'in a moment pattern' see book 1/2 – expectation and preparation primed)

you **feel relaxed, calm and safe...**

something is changing

making you **feel much better...**

as you **calm down, you feel better** *all over...*

perhaps **there is a changing sensation** *in that part?*

Maybe it feels warmer?

Or just better in some way?

You can feel that pleasant sensation growing already...

Comfort *is spreading...*

Comfort *is growing...*

That **part** *can* **feel so comfortable...**

That part feels so comfortable...

You **feel calm**, *rested and relaxed as that occurs...*

You **feel comfortable** *all over...*

Very pleasant as your **pleasing sensations only grow, now...**

(If you want: elicit a colour of comfort and give suggestions for it to spread where needed – see 'colour feelings' in book 1 'How to hypnotise anyone,' and 2 'Mastering hypnotic language.' End hypnosis with 'permanency suggestion.')

These **pleasant feelings can remain with you** *from now on.'*

Here's an even shorter script for rapid pain removal.

Superman pain script.

(Hypnosis assumed or you can do waking hypnosis)

'**Focus** *on that pain....*

You are in charge of that...

Visualise where that pain is inside

explore where it is in your mind's eye...

notice where any inflammation/injury is...

Imagine that like superman

you have x ray powers!

So you can easily

see all the anatomical structure of it...

Picture it, *vividly....clearly...*

Now...

Let it go...

Let it melt...

Let it evaporate...

Let it fade...

Let it diminish...

Watch that **feeling go away completely...** ´

(*Troubleshooting:* you can place their hand on that part, put a cool cloth on it, whatever, not needed but you could: this will help draw attention to that part. You can also get them to imagine a control panel that lowers pain levels etc. If a technique doesn't work say, 'That's fine. Let's try this.' **Clients are in my experience very understanding.**)

The moment it sinks in.

I'll leave you with a principle of waking hypnosis – let's call it the **'moment of recognition/realization';** this is when your suggestion sinks in, the person gets it, the subconscious knows what to do. The look is, and many other experienced hypnotists have spoken about it, just the same as when you say something like, 'You know what a donkey looks like?' and they have a look of 'I do.'

Some people just say 'Uhu.' So they get what a donkey is etc. The look you don't want is a screwed up face which says, 'What?!'

Limited vision.

Dr. Milton Erickson discovered way back in the 1930s that people in waking hypnosis can only see so far; if on a stage they only saw Erickson and no crowd. If he directed their attention to the crowd they saw sections of it but no back wall or sides of the auditorium. You can check for genuine waking hypnosis by asking a person what their field of view is.

Are you feeling sheepy? TV zombies!

Ok let's just cut the nonsense and get down to why TV is SO bad for you.

- It without any shadow of a doubt covertly hypnotises you.

- It standardises culture globally and creates conformity, thereby eventually destroying indigenous cultures. This is known as 'cultural diffusion.' It is a form of genocide strictly speaking.

- It lowers the self-esteem of watchers by forcing them to compare themselves to impossible ideals of perfection; women are especially at risk of this. Growing incidents of anorexia in boys suggests generation X/Yers are being affected more than their predecessors.

- It wastes life time: it is passive living. Get off your fat arse and **bite into the arse of life** you couch zombie! To be vitally alive you must

DO SOMETHING! <u>Make things happen.</u>

- What you consume/ingest including visually and auditorily becomes manifest in you: whether you let in junk food or junk culture it will affect you mood, life choices and behaviour in general. *You are what you watch and listen to.*

- Unlike reading which demands active participation and thinking/work, TV doesn't even demand you be fully awake! TV is something that is done <u>to</u> you. Ever noticed how people doze off in front of TV?

- It engenders people to watch and participate in a fake 'TV world' culture that only exists on sound stages/studios/C.G.I programmer's desk tops. People are therefore less likely to create their own culture: through painting, their own forms of dance, their own native social rituals and their own folk music.

- It increases a sense of isolation: people used to talk to neighbours about things that were going on; now they stare at the 'goggle-box!' It is getting worse now as younger people, even women lose social skills because they are semi-permanently attached to some confounded piece of technology. People are not communicating face to face – when we communicate face to face we can see the whole person, we can see when they are genuine or deceptive, we can spot their charming idiosyncrasies like the way a girl wiggles her nose or curls the corner of her mouth up at the side etc. **GET AWAY FROM THE BOX AND TALK TO REAL PEOPLE!** Seriously folks some researchers are finding that people who are overly engrossed in TV, online media, you name it are becoming more 'autistic.'

- On the old TVs the flicker rate would induce waking hypnosis in the viewer, with the newer TVs the 'pulse rate' does it apparently?! Why would you build a technology with the intention of willfully inducing waking hypnosis????!

- TV is addictive. *Anything that can focus your mind on it is potentially addictive.* Addiction has many qualities that are highly similar to hypnotic phenomena. TV like computer games, virtual reality etc. allow the fed up, the depressed and the just common all garden miserable to **become absorbed** into the la-la land of fantasy TV offers. But like all drugs she never delivers and drawing you away from reality she ensures you never get your real needs met. TV is a cheap slut.

- It causes stress, anxiety, depression and PTSD (Post Traumatic Stress Disorder); yes you can be traumatised by watching gruesome events on the box: fact. I had a client who told me she had been deeply disturbed by watching the gruesome killing of former Libyan tyrant Colonel Gadhafi which was widely aired on prime time news globally.

- It destroys regional accents. It creates a globalised 'Trans-Atlantic' English.

- TV exposes the watcher's eyes to an unnatural amount of artificial light; ***the consequences of this exposure are unknown.*** Short sightedness is known to be caused by living in environments in which there is a limited viewing space.

- It encourages a sense of unreality and fantasy about what is desirable or possible in waking life. It therefore induces delusional belief patterns. I have noticed all very young children want to be famous – why? The whole family sits around that box and stares at it. The child concludes consciously and unconsciously that in this culture to be watched is to be important. And conversely that anonymity is 'extinction.'

- Like the imagination which is in part a virtual reality simulator, the TV installs 'others' imaginative creations rather than the viewer creating their own. Porn, erotic literature (porn for women – 'Romance fiction' my a**e ladies) – you name it. I will give scientific proof of this later in the book. <u>Fantasy literally rewires the brain cells.</u>

- There is evidence that the passivity of the brain during TV exposure may lead in later life to Alzheimer's. As the brain ages it needs to be used to stay healthy.

- It leads to obesity, bad posture, a bad back, laying or sitting for unnaturally long periods of time. Go exercise – you'll feel amazing and reduce stress.

- It makes you stupid and ignorant. I
  have met clients (men) who told me
  they only like 'facts.' They all said
  they like watching the Discovery
  and History channel more than
  anything else. Rii-iight! 'Factual
  channels' are a joke, they're for
  kids. Try reading a book, just one
  and thinking!

- Related to above: children who
  watch a great deal of TV lack social
  and communication skills gained
  from playing with other children and
  adults for that matter. Don't let the
  TV be your kid's baby-sitter. For a
  brief stint I worked in TV folks, the
  former head of BBC's children's
  programming said, 'It's not our job
  to educate the little shits, it's our
  job to entertain them.' That's your
  little shits she was talking about.
  The media is full of weirdoes.

- It increases a sense of frustration:
  programmes like Dallas were
  'beamed' into the former Soviet
  Union to create a 'grass is greener'

mentality. However 'programmers' also do this in the West to Westerners. TV is responsible for creating the 'keeping up with the Jones's' mentality. This is aimed at women, then the family get in debt.

- It encourages mindless consumerism, crass materialism and shopping addiction. You can tell what is important to a society by its architecture. Where I live the shopping mall is the biggest focal point outside of residential suburban areas; what about where you live?

- It makes the insignificant significant. Many losers, half-wits and ne'er do wells have been raised to the undeserved status of idols thanks to TV. The worship of the mundane as opposed to the inspirational effects of great art degrades human culture making it vapid and nihilistic.

- It turns your into a sheeple-zombie. Don't believe me? Look around you folks – ask yourself **DO MOST PEOPLE REALLY LOOK AWAKE OR IN A DAZE?** Let me ask you a question: what meaning does TV have in your life? It's just a box, a screen right? There was a song, *'I was sitting with Matthew, we were watching TV I said; Hey Matthew, what do you see? Do you see the guns? Do you see the bombs? See those people throwing all of those stones? Do you see the cars going up in flames? See their faces, do you know their names? Hey Matthew, when you're watching TV; Hey, Hey Matthew, what do you see?'*

WHAT DO **YOU** SEE?

'Approved by the FDA, MHRA' is a waking suggestion.

If you read a medicine label or see a advertised treatment and it says 'approved/recommended by the Food and Drug Administration (FDA)' or its equivalent in the UK the Medicines and Healthcare products Regulatory Agency (MHRA) and National Institute for Health and Clinical Excellence (NICE), you are highly likely to act upon it as a positive suggestion even though it may well cause iatrogenic disease; that is illness caused by medical examination or treatment!!! A third of all deaths in the USA and UK EVERY YEAR are caused by iatrogenic disease or rather your doctor's actions or more specifically the 'Big Pharma' medicine he/she prescribes killing you or maiming you. So it's the third biggest killer!!! It causes at a low end estimate 225,000 deaths a year in the US! That's a massacre by anyone's rational estimation!

These are the costs per year according to one study...

- 116 million extra physician visits.

- 77 million extra prescriptions.

- 17 million emergency department visits.

- 8 million hospitalizations.

- 3 million long-term admissions.

- 199,000 additional deaths.

- $77 billion in extra costs.

(Sources for these figures in this module: Journal of the American Medical Association, Harvard University, Centers for Disease Control, British Medical Journal, The Lancet, New England Journal of Medicine and National News, New York Times, Washington Post, CNN, US World Report.)

All the doctors in the UK do after diagnosing you is look in a big drug book, thumb through it and say, 'Yes that one will do.' It is well known that doctors are given free gifts and free holidays etc. by the big drug companies. **There is an iron-clad law of persuasion and influence – 'reciprocity' a.k.a. 'You scratch my back and I'll scratch yours.'** When people, and almost all businesses do it, give you FREE STUFF you feel a natural human *obligation* to return the favour.

To conclude: the person most likely to 'kill' you (accidentally obviously)? Your doctor!!!? The way I see medicines is like this: ever seen a sheep dip? We are the sheep; herd level medicines are used rather than ones tailored specifically to the individual's genome. This is why so many medicines produce terrible reactions in people – you are just a statistic to the makers.

And people are worried about hypnosis???! *They already ARE hypnotised!*

Please don't take this section as an attack on the Medical Profession, doctors do a lot of good and have saved more lives than I ever will, if your body is broken go see a Doc. Modern medicine has in recent years made some breath-taking advances in repairing physical damage.

Rapid pain relief using waking hypnosis for children.

Try this with children in pain or adapt it for adults. *Children believe in magic.* Use that to your advantage. Speak in concrete, simple words. The embeds are not needed, they are included as an option.

Magic medicine script.

'Would you like some of my 'magic medicine?'

It will **make it all better, now...**
(expectation)

Ok I have some in my hand...

I'm just going to rub it on x (x being anywhere – it could be directly on the injury etc.)

You'll feel it working soon... (in a moment pattern)

Can you **feel it now?**

In a few moment's **you'll feel a tingling.**

The feeling of the tingling can magically

spread

to where it would make you **feel best of all.**

This pleasant tingling is all you feel, now...

Just **feel that lovely pleasant tingling...**

Now, **that feels better doesn't it?**
('That' – dissociative).

Ok, you did fantastically! (Always praise successful change work especially with tiddlers.)

Can you put out your hand for me?

Lovely.

I am going to give you enough magic medicine

to last as long as you need it.

Anytime you need it

just rub in the magic medicine and **feel**

better again.

Ok? Good.'

(Obviously look for cues from the child/client that this is indeed occurring. Look for the 'moment of recognition etc.')

The neon sign deepener.

I adapted this from a ye olde practitioner of hypnosis. Throw it in when/where it seems appropriate – it utilises imagination, shapes (symbols) and the implication of going down.

The neon sign deepener script.

(Hypnosis assumed)

*'Simply **imagine** a bright neon sign in your mind's eye...*

get to know that sign...

What does it say?

Is it anything of importance or just random?

What colour is it?

Pink?

A luminous yellowy-green?

How big is that sign?

Ok.

All of a sudden the neon sign blinks and goes out

as if there has been a power cut...

and just as suddenly a bright neon square appears

where that sign once was...

What colour is that square?

How big is it?

How bright is it?

Notice all its qualities.

Now,

a capital letter 'A' appears in the centre of that square...

look at that 'A,'

is it big or small?

Is it bright or dim?

Before you know it,

that A fizzles out

and a capital letter 'B' appears in neon...

Again what colour is that 'B'?

Get to know it,

it's shape, size,

it's brightness or dimness...

Now as I count **down** *from 20-0 you can*

keep seeing those letters appearing and disappearing

not yet but soon when I start the count

you'll see in turn

'C'

'D'

'E'

they'll all appear and disappear in turn...

so as you go from C-Z...

watching those changing letters,

those symbols of human communication

you can notice with each new letter...

you **become more hypnotically**

absorbed

and ***more deeply relaxed***

as you head closer and closer to Z

*each letter will **relax** you more and more*

so that by the time I reach 0

no matter what letter in the alphabet you got to

*you'll be very **deeply and profoundly relaxed***

*in a deep state of hypnosis and **a deep state of trance...***

now...

Ok let's start...

See that 'C' appear in 'Bs' place rapidly

and 20

*19 **going deeper***

18 and 17 and 16

15 deeper...

*More relaxed and **more intensely hypnotised** with each changing letter...*

14

13

12, and how deep does your unconscious want you to go today?

11

10

*9 even more **deeply entranced and hypnotised** with each succeeding letter...*

those changing letters...

and letters make up powerful words of change...

8

7

6 even more so

5 won't it be wonderful to

feel that growing feeling of hypnosis and trance, now?

4

3 almost there

2 and 1

You are almost where you desire to be, unconsciously, now

0

You are deeply hypnotised

deeply relaxed

in deep hypnotic sleep!

And just before we move on

you see that last letter you saw...

that took you this deep...

change to a certain symbol

that has deep, positive and profound meaning for you...

and as soon as you see that meaningful

symbol...

(Pause a moment)

you ***go even deeper than before, now...***

There IS evil waking hypnosis!

Apart from the daily verbal abuse which many people suffer and which causes psychological and physiological stress responses there is another type of evil waking hypnosis – **the malediction; or as it is more popularly known - the curse.** The stuff of legend in folklore of witches and gypsies? No; it is a documented fact. Some highly suggestible people can be 'killed' by a curse. There are records of one woman placing a freezing curse on a man who spent the next 20 years wrapped up in bed complaining of the cold. Another story tells how a pair of boys caught stealing vegetables from a man's farm were cursed to die from the sensation of a painful spike: one of the boys became rapidly ill with unexplained stomach pain and died soon after. These aren't tall tales from paranormal websites; these are taken from 19th century medical records in the United States/UK.

On a lighter note: that reminds me of voodoo…

Freaky voodoo sex doll: that naughty man molested my Barbie!

I once saw a perv-notist hypnotise a woman. In his hand he held an innocuous looking Barbie doll. Its hair disheveled yes but otherwise innocent enough. He then gave the hypnotised woman (who wore a skimpy bikini) the suggestion that every time he rubbed Barbie's 'private parts' that the woman would feel it as though it were happening to her and be accordingly aroused. The woman's chair grinding and pleasurable moaning suggested it worked!!! Dirty pervnosis! Quite funny though.

Her eyes were open so technically she was in waking hypnosis at that stage. So how do you hypnotise someone but get them to open their eyes and still remain entranced? Easy.

'In a moment I'll click my fingers (do x – x being any trigger) *and your eyes will open but you will remain in this state: in deep, relaxed hypnosis feeling wonderful.'*

If you are worried if certain suggestions are acceptable to certain people just say,

'You'll of course only act upon suggestions you find acceptable.'

This of course suggests the above woman was a wanton slut. Now where did I put her number???

Why people turn to 'alternative therapies.'

In a nutshell: because they think with good reason they won't harm or kill them. Did you know that lemon juice from a fresh lemon when applied to acne lesions will often remove them and lead to clear skin far faster than any over the counter potion you could purchase at a local chemist? Who would have thunked it?! The previous statement is not to be taken as medical advice: if you do anything I write about in this book you are responsible not me. I accept no liability thanks very much! People with dark skin should not use it, it can bleach it.

It does seem that nature has many cures secreted amongst her plant life. The trouble is finding out where! I don't see modern medicine as the prime choice of treatment for a wide array of problems; there are many better, safer treatments. The word 'alternative' is pure 'psycho-linguistics' used by the medical profession to solidify their hegemony over all available treatment modalities. As I have gotten older I have come to the conclusion that Dr. Johnson, the man who compiled the first English Dictionary was right in saying, 'Any man who is not his own doctor by the age of 40 is a fool!'

If you have seen the film Lorenzo's Oil or even heard about the true life story behind it, you'll know patients and their families CAN and do find cures for themselves when modern medicine fails to do so. A patient is someone who passively waits to be cured. A client is someone fully engaged in the healing process, they are playing an active role in it.

Street hypnosis exposed: beginner's level!

What the hell in heck IS street hypnosis anyway? It is a version of waking stage hypnosis although you do it in a shopping centre/mall or out in the open somewhere, if that's how you get your kicks. That's pretty much it. Apparently it's more 'cool,' ahem – riiiiight! It totally bores me but I know how to do it. It uses rapid inductions and is much like a magic show. Magic is hypnotic. The hypnotist plays with the hypnotee and exerts his 'power' over them to 'get them' to do pretty much what he wants them to. All the usual rules of hypnosis apply. I'll teach you how to make someone have anything stick to their fingers.

- Script first, principles second: get a pen, a sheet of paper, anything; this is your hypno-prop.

- Tell the sucker you are a Master Hypnotist – don't say pwetty pwease can I try this pwease.

- Use any other tricks in this book to set up a 'hypnotic mood,' check for somnambulists etc.

- Before doing this gimmick you can idea seed by talking about sticky things etc., thereby directionalising and priming the mind.

Street hypnosis hand stick script.

(Get victim to hold prop with arm outstretched. EMBEDS NOT REQUIRED)

'Like to **do something hypnotic?**

(Victim says, 'Sure, yes etc.,' they wouldn't be there otherwise right?)

Ok, that's it...just hold that like that... (truism of ongoing reality as you give 'em the prop)

Concentrate your focus on x (Focus 1: External. X = prop)

and on your breathing... (Focus 2: Internal)

pay attention... (To what??!)

breathe easy...

and **feel that hand squeezing/sticking to x etc...**

Only **in your mind** *repeat your favourite tune over and over again...*

(Focus 3: Internal)

Repeat that tune over and over again...

Now <u>*TRY*</u> *to release the x but notice to your delighted surprise...*

(Law of reversed effort – the harder you try the less you can do it)

as you continue to hum that tune...

<u>*TRYING*</u> *to let the x fall*

as **it sticks tighter and tighter to that hand...**

glued solidly, **becoming more and more stuck**

with each passing moment.'

So how does this hypno-gimmick work? Well, it...

- Uses expectation of hypnosis.

- Your and their hypnotic intent.

- Focuses the mind on multiple tasks thus overloading it.

- Focusing on breathing is inherently hypnotic.

- It sends the person inside (humming) and outside at once (non-verbal apposition of opposites) splitting consciousness. This makes someone distracted, seeking 'rebalance' (it's confusing) and so they are suggestible to instructions in order to find the desired 'rebalance.'

- You can get someone to recite the alphabet backwards, anything. I even heard of a man who gets his victims to say, 'I will drop this x,' over and over. Try stuff out and see what works for you. Be brave, experiment on friends etc. Or you can do a 'rapid sensory shift,' e.g. *'Remember a time you were seeing something beautiful – what sounds are there too?'* Or use a 'pseudo-negation' to create confusion, 'Recall a time you where tasting something delicious. What sights were you ignoring?' **Just occupy that mind with something odd.**

- You need to be word perfect like an actor to do this stuff: practise on a Barbie doll or stick of celery in your bedroom first.

I will cover street hypnosis in much more depth in a later book; this is just to whet your appetite. *If you don't fancy street hypnosis just remember the hypnotic principles involved. You can use them elsewhere or notice where else they are being used against you.*

'Fair seeming tongues': evil is revealed in the voice.

Evil people have evil voices. They pretend to be kind and fair but underneath is a not so subtly veiled cruelty, a deep callousness. Sometimes you can almost smell the brimstone! I once heard an interview with a 'hitman' shall we say; his smoky voice reeked of pure, unadulterated evil, it was unmistakable, the superficial charm was swamped by a studied intonation of danger. Such fiends will often rationalise their evil and make it seem normal, lucid and quite reasonable – because to them it is! Evil voices are unmistakable, listen out for them. All psychopaths have one.

The phobia removal super suggestion.

Once I have removed a phobia through either symbology as I do now or as I used to with my own NLP phobia cure (see it in full later in this book) I decided I needed a good 'wrapping up' super suggestion – just to tidy any possible loose ends. It's short and sweet. Remember you almost always have to have done something else first to get rid of the unnecessary fear, although is possible to just use suggestion to get rid of fears, it's been done...

Phobia super suggestion module.

'There is no fear of x, (specific phobia)

no fear of y (etc.)

no panic, just calm now...

no fear of fear because those old responses

are for panicky, phobic people (this is a perceived 'identity level' suggestion, deeper than mere 'behaviour level' ones)

and (client's name) *isn't one of those.*

No problem whatsoever:

he/she is strong, confident, courageous and

at ease when he/she needs to be.

No animal, object, process, (here begins the removal of ALL 'silly' fears)

procedure or profession,

bodily function:

no problem whatsoever.

Emotion, open or enclosed space

or place, elevation, height

or vehicle or speed:

no problem whatsoever!

Type of person,

regardless of status, (the client's or anyone else's)

many, few or none,

old or young, (multiple meanings: others' age and throughout client's life etc. – the subconscious processes ALL possible meanings)

man or woman –

no problem whatsoever!

Nor natural event or occasion

bother you from now on. (Healthy, essential fear is not removed only phobic fear – the subconscious can differentiate you know!)

You are fearless,   (state this boldly – as a fact!)

scared of nothing –

inside or out,

at any time

or environment,

whoever you are with

and no matter what the sex,

position or numbers or not: (sexually ambiguous in case of nervousness in that department plus has non-sexual meanings too/don't be afraid of appropriate sexual metaphor it can be used to evoke surprise/shock)

no problem whatsoever.

Now,

you walk through this world with confidence,

courage, ease!

Unnecessary fear is gone:

save it for _real_ danger from now on.
(Emphasise the world _real._)

Balanced, stable

solid – confidence!

You have unlearned what you had learned.'
(I like this, sounds a bit Yoda-ry)

As an end note: I hate it when people call phobias 'irrational' fears – it implies insanity. Phobias are not irrational – they are sane responses and warning signs of stress, overload and high background anxiety levels. They are signs of psychological pain! Anxiety is brain pain!

'Emoto-nosis': how intense emotions hypnotise you.

Intense emotions of varying kinds 'swamp' the brain causing 'black and white' thinking and totally shut down the 'higher brain' (thinking and critical part). Anything that shuts down the analytical factor opens the mind to suggestion and worse, programming. Firstly let's examine the obvious emotions: fear and anger.

Fright night!

When in a state of **fear** you are in a hypnotic state and are therefore VERY suggestible. Think how people jump at scary movies but nothing really happened! Good for taking girls to because they cling to you for comfort ;)

Hulk smash!!!

Are you an **anger**-holic? When angry, lashing out, blaming whoever for whatever you are in a highly focused, unthinking, emotional state – in fact you have generated a powerful hypnotic state. Cults and brainwashers try to make people angry or scared because then they become programmable.

If in any cult-like situation you must remain calm. This is why Pavlov discovered that the more temperamentally phlegmatic, calm dogs were harder to condition. There is a story about a man who wished to become a Methodist and attended many of their meetings hoping to have his moment of speaking in tongues, having a hysterical 'conversion fit' etc. as the preacher promised fire and brimstone to the mob. It never worked, why? He was so calm by nature that he couldn't be riled up.

Interestingly bullies (who have overly high self-worth no matter what do-gooder cr*p you've heard) intentionally provoke fear/anger so that the victim cannot respond rationally.

Love is all you need.

But my young padawans, what is THE most powerful emoto-nosis state? Women will probably get this first. **Love**, you big dummy! Lovenosis can move mountains!!! What happens when you love someone? You absorb everything about them. Their facial expressions, movements, small habits, the way they play with their hair in that way. You think everything they say is wonderful and fascinating. What is one of my favourite embeds? Hands up. Yes, I say – **become absorbed;** as we do, when in love. 'Deeply' in love is a giveaway folks. Think of the love of a close and loving family. What wouldn't they do for one another?

The green-eyed monster.

Jealousy is another VERY hypnotic state. Think of Othello and how the psychopath Iago actually uses hypnosis, reframing and innuendo to paint entirely fake pictures in the play's namesake's head. Pathological jealousy is the subject of the film 'Raging Bull' starring Robert De Niro. In the movie Rocky Marciano works himself into hypnodial fits of paranoid raging jealousy while his wife is actually completely loyal. His wild, raving misuse of his imagination and low self-worth lead him to reframe every action of his innocent wife into a sign of non-existent infidelity; tragically unable to change he drifts into a dead end of loneliness. 'Beware my lord of jealousy...'

You have sinned!

Guilt/remorse: is another one; see religious hypnosis and girlfriend hypnosis. Girls from an early age are masters of guiltnosis: whereby they make you feel guilty when you didn't do ANYTHING wrong. Elicited by brainwashers to create the highly emotional 'conversation state.' See the section on cults.

Much hate I sense in you...

Hate; remember 1984 by Orwell (if you haven't read it you must) Winston and all citizens of air strip one (formerly England) are compelled to attend a daily 'Hate' or the two minute hate as it is known. At a packed cinema the low level Party operatives must shout and hurl abuse at pictures of the 'enemy' – the fictitious 'Goldstein' who embodies all heretical evil and anyone who 'supports him' by being against the Party, to whatever degree.

Orwell described the lunacy of the Hate as an extreme act so weird *'that **a child should have been able to see through it.'** He adds that it is, '... just **plausible enough,'** to create an alarmed feeling so that other people stupid, gullible, irrational folks would be drawn in. Children would see through the Hate. Not yet culturally hypnotised they can easily see through nonsense that adults can't.

Waking hypnotic principles in the daily Hate?

1. Cinema.

2. Plausible ritual.

2. Mob.

3. Frenzied emotional state.

4. Repetitive, ritual behaviour.

5. N.A.C (Neuro-Associative-Conditioning) to images of the 'scapegoat.' See book 3, 'Powerful hypnosis,' for a detailed breakdown of N.A.C.

Ever heard the saying – '...he was **consumed** by hate,' ?

Attraction is not a choice.

Attraction to another person is a great inducer of waking hypnosis. You have to keep looking at them – *fixation of attention,* and they induce a powerful and pleasurable altered state. You know what the main factor in attraction is? Availability, proximity – that is it! You know what mitigates against it? Perceived low social value. Women with self-perceived high social status will rarely make the beast with two backs with men they see as socially subordinate to them except to p**s off an overly strict daddy or ex-boyfriend.

Attraction is closely followed by...

I'm just your average horny little devil.

Lust obviously is a powerfully and potentially compulsive state. It can consume your focus totally and create drug-like states of sexual intoxication. Believe it or not when in a hyper-aroused state of lust you are both programmable AND highly hypnotisable. Beware of porn!!! Do you know archaeology seems to have proven that people are naturally monogamous? Do you know which creature highly sexually promiscuous people act like? Baboons.

Gigglenosis?

Laughter; when you laugh you are open somewhat, if shocked and you laugh you are suggestible. People are more open to change their mind in normal circumstances when they feel good. Resistance goes down: maybe this is the reason men can, 'laugh women into bed.'

What do all these states and more have in common? As a consequence people want to take **_action_** one way or another. Now, no one has ever manipulated these emoto-hypnosis states in real life, have they????! What do you think?

Pain: some people who have been abused learn to associate pain with orgasm. A rare few can't have an orgasm through normal sex. They can have it through experiencing pain. This must have been programmed in during childhood abuse. This is how masochists are hypnotically created. I can't reveal my source for this, it's too Twin-Peaks to go into!

Creating cliffhangers and nested loops.

Let's deal with so-called 'Nested loops' (it's such a vile, soulless NLP term); folks they're just cliff-hangers. When I was little boy there was much more choice on TV. The BBC would put on the old Buster Crab Flash Gordon and Buck Rogers cinema serials. At the end of every show Flash Gordon or the heroine would be left in some terrible danger and you had to watch next week to find out if he/she survived the onslaught of the Mudmen or that giant walking Lobster creature! The film-makers had hooked you – you wanted to see the completion of the tale. This is how 'nested loops' work.

I wrote a therapeutic cliff-hanger once to help a man who kept coming back to see me again and again. He was one of my 'What about Bob?' clients. There follows 3 stories threaded together. They are intentionally left incomplete and the subconscious opens up a 'completion template' that longs for the tale to be resolved, creating 'response potential' (see book 1). As the subconscious sees the stories as significant to itself it eagerly awaits the story's continuation and completion. You could use this technique any way you want: you could start the first part of the story at the beginning of a hypnosis session, you could do some other change work and then come back to the tale etc., etc., 'fractionating' the story on and off.

Therapeutic cliff-hangers script for generic habit change.

'There was once a boy who wanted to learn to ride a bike,

it was shiny and red and yellow,

he loved that bike, he really wanted to learn to ride it,

he knew that it represented his growing up,

his developing sense of **maturity and independence...**

And there was a man who wanted to **stop doing something**

that he knew wasn't good for him.

It was just some dumb habit he'd gotten into the **habit** *of and he wanted to* **change...**

And there was a woman who came to see me

about stopping smoking and she didn't believe it was possible

to **stop something like that, permanently**...*so I just started talking to her...*

And the boy was out riding

and he fell over and grazed his knee

and he even crashed into a tree but he never stopped,

he got up, dusted himself down and tried again,

and as they say **practise makes perfect**

because

he really wanted to ride that bike

and soon enough he was an expert...

how he enjoyed riding that red and yellow bike...

And that man tried and he **stopped that**

thing *for a while*

and then it would just come back...

and again he'd be successful

and yet that habit came back

and really he realised that he had to

make a decision,

commit to it and stick to it 100%

with complete determination to change permanently,

and when he did,

make that decision,

all of his unconscious forces,

powers,

abilities really did come to his aid, just like that...

And after just one session

that woman stopped smoking,

because

she discovered the power of her own inner mind

to help her **change and it just happened just like that**

and I didn't even do much, because she did all the rest, ***now...'***

(Get the idea? Easy isn't it – as you can see I prefer to call this device, 'therapeutic cliff-hangers.' They are just a variant of ordinary therapeutic metaphors, as they are more complex they create overload and natural amnesia.)

Mythical structure matches therapeutic structure.

Joseph Campbell the great comparative mythologist identified 3 phases/stages to the mythic heroes quest and to religious initiation.

1. Person is separated from normal environment.

2. Transformative process occurs.

3. Individual is reintegrated to society with 'new' resources, learnings.

This matches the structure of hypnotherapy.

1. Person leaves their 'normal' life and goes to therapist's office etc.

2. Hypnotherapy occurs: a trance-formative process.

3. Individual returns to world 'healed.'

Wery interwesting!!! *This reminds me of a principle of behaviourism: change the environment or something in it and you can change behaviour.* The home computer is a powerful example of this: it's transformed our lives!

Hypnotically soulless: how to spot a psychopath!

Why are we even talking about psychopaths in a book on hypnosis? Because psychopaths have instinctive hypnotic power over real humans. Because as a hypnotherapist we treat human suffering; the major cause of human suffering throughout human history has been and is the action/s of psychopaths. It is absolutely essential you know about them. There is a fascination with true evil in all human cultures. The source? Psychopaths.

- Psychopaths often have 'messiah' complexes. This is not to infer that the historical 'Jesus' was one; he most certainly was NOT! They want to change the world and everything and everyone in it.

- Psychopaths have a 'spell-binding' effect on most non-psychopaths.

- They can spot each other in a crowd. Just like the film, 'They Live,' which is excellent, you should see it if you haven't.

- Psychopaths are charming. Superficially.

- They have a bad sense of smell compared to real humans.

- They have a need for constant stimulation and entertainment: they don't sit and quietly reflect.

- ***Psychopaths fear exposure more than anything.***

- Not all psychopaths kill or torture others. Some do it indirectly.

- They lie as often as others breathe. They lie flawlessly and without ANY guilt.

- They see manipulation as fine and dandy: anything can be used – NLP, hypnosis, violence, the creation of pseudo guilt, 'gas lighting,' you name it.

- The indicators of psychopathy and what was called 'demonic possession' are identical.

- They feel ZERO guilt or remorse for wrongdoing.

- They are parasitic: they live off of others. Recently in my area a psychopath 'rentboy' lived off a poor old lonely man stealing all his money gradually; when he had bled his victim dry, he killed him by beating him to death. This is clearly one of the origins of the vampire myth: sucking others' blood in order to live.

- They are callous; they have NO empathy for others in any way, shape or form.

- In repose they have hooded eyes.

- Sexually promiscuity, weak behaviour control.

- Psychopaths are common not rare: look for them in high-powered board rooms more often than with society's dregs. The stupid ones become low-level criminals and thugs, the more intelligent ones become 'white-collar' criminals.

- They have delusional goals: they are usually unattainable to the low influence ones because the psychopath is a talentless loser.

- Impulsive or irresponsible behaviour.

- Unable to sustain long-term relationships. There are frequently a string of short term marriages and failed relationships in their wake.

- Killing and torturing animals habitually as a child. Not just a one off, a pattern is needed.

- Although they may well get caught for their crimes eventually, often due to their snakelike cunning, they get away with many more.

- Juvenile delinquency and being in trouble as a youngster are often indications of psychopathy. Women like bad boys. Hmmmm?

- They often claim to be hard done by and judged too harshly by others – a kind of 'woe is me,' 'why can't I get a break,' mentality. They use this to gain sympathy in order to exploit. A great example of this kind of psychopath is the original 'Brimstone and Treacle' TV film written by Dennis Potter (not the one with Sting who is bloody awful!)

- They look for highly competitive environments in which utter ruthlessness 'cheating,' and outright criminality are a prerequisite: City of London, Wall Street, politics. Researchers claim that acting and directing are also professions they are attracted to: **where there is power potential and risk potential you will find a psychopath.** You get the idea. They are 'highly functional.'

- They are totally dead on the inside: they appreciate no awe of nature, no true joy inspired by art. **They hate beauty but can be captivated by it.**

- They have no problems sleeping at night. Nothing worries them.

- They have an inflated sense of 'entitlement' because they feel so superior to real humans.

- They believe they are perfect.

- Pritchard referred to these monsters as 'morally insane.'

- They live only in the present: they take what they want: now! Anyone who opposes or presents an obstacle to this 'nowness' is an enemy and therefore bad. In the present 'culture' 'live in the now' is a common mindless slogan that people parrot. Hmmmm?

- They often pass polygraph tests as they have little if any physiological stress responses to lying – no sweat or tremors; nothing.

- They study real humans fully: they know which 'buttons' to press. They start studying real humans from a very early age.

- They speak in terms of emotionless cause and effect when telling of their crimes.

- They know full well that they traumatise humans just by their evil presence. They use this to achieve aims. This quality 'psychologically stuns' their victims. Think of cobras etc.

- They can fool other psychopaths, psychiatrists: given the right circumstances they can fool almost everyone.

- When caught committing crimes they seek to focus investigators minds on *THEIR* lack of essential needs being met.

- According to Michael Woodworth, a psychologist who studies psychopathy at the University of British Columbia, 'It is unbelievable...You can spend two or three hours (interviewing psychopaths) and come out feeling like you are hypnotized.' We shall examine this soon.

- They use more 'dysfluencies' - the 'uhs and 'ums' that interrupt speech, to *seem* normal: also known as 'the mask of sanity.'

- They often refer to crimes in the past tense – showing detachment.

- Psychopaths' languaging contain more words known as 'subordinating conjunctions.' These words, including 'because, before, although, as etc.' are associated with cause-and-effect statements. Psychos seem to see the world *only* as simple cause and effect.

- Often truly talented people, top brains in any field do what they do because it arouses such passion. Note: psychopaths are only capable of a superficial understanding of any subject. Passion is a normal and healthy human trait; psychopaths lack it totally.

- They are wholly materialistic using twice as many words related to basic physiological needs and self-preservation, including eating, drinking and money.

- They use less emotionally intense language than real humans. Although they will often talk a lot about emotions and having them; unlike a real person who just *has* emotions. They will use words like 'passionate.' They do get angry when challenged.

- Family, religion, self-worth are an irrelevancy: they are connected to nothing higher than themselves. Although they claim to have unmet needs they have wholly non-human needs.

- A crime to a psychopath in psychopath logic is simply a series of logical steps to achieve their 'goals.' And the ends always justify the means.

- They are a bit like the Android in the first Alien film. They fake what they see as 'appropriate emotions' in response to events: smiling when others receive good news, looking sad if someone's cat dies, or mournful at a funeral BUT they will then make sexual advances toward a widow.

- Knowing they are different from early childhood they mimic others normal behaviour to escape detection. They do not want or desire to behave as real humans do but they recognise for the majority of the time that they must.

- *A lack of pity is essential for power* – psychopaths rise easily to the top of human social hierarchies; this is much easier for them in civilised societies than in primitive ones. Psychopaths in at least one primitive culture are referred to as 'those who sleep with our wives while we are hunting.' They are usually taken out on a hunt and killed by the tribal males.

- If attacked or exposed psychos seek to destroy a person through subtle insidious means: they will download child abuse images and send them to your email etc. They will use slander, innuendo etc.

- They enjoy humiliating, belittling, mistreating, deriding, attacking, killing those that they perceive as being weaker than themselves: they are the ultimate 'Social Darwinists.' The old, children, disabled etc. are fair game. It is interesting that so many 'talent' (actually lack of talent) shows have this kind of relationship between 'judge' and 'contestant.'

- They never admit mistakes or accept responsibility for wrong doing: it is always the victim's fault. The psycho always had the best of intentions; from their own perspective of course. If powerful they will say things like, 'I just did what I had to do to get the job done.'

- Someone who is not psychopathic but acts like one is known as a 'secondary psychopath.' These are those who perceive that psychopaths and their traits are to be emulated as they lead to 'success.' They may do this entirely unconsciously. *There are many of these people about.*

- They show no or very little (faked) emotion to real trauma or life stressors.

- In private many police officers and doctors (psychiatrists) who have to deal with these creatures say they'd lose their jobs if they told the public about this but that they know that a psychopath is not a true human being in any sense of the word.

- Women find psychopathic traits attractive. This is a generalisation but nonetheless true.

- Psychopaths are attracted to extreme ideologies. They often create them. The 'ideology' gives a pseudo-rational to non-psychopaths as to why they must suffer etc.

- All psychopaths think they are better than everyone else and better at doing anything than anyone else.

- Psychopaths can see through a con.

- Psychopaths know they are different from a very early age.

- Psychopaths call normal people 'empaths.'

- When violent revolutions occur around the world psychopaths flood there en masse to get involved in the violence and tyranny that will ensue.

- Psychopaths are very vain and narcissistic. In the myth, Narcissus fell in love with his own reflection NOT his true self. They deny their true self: it is dead for all intents and purposes.

- Psychopaths change personas rapidly and at various stages of life; so they do not accept responsibility for what various earlier 'incarnations' have done – as they see it – 'they' didn't do it.

- They have very warped goals from a real human's point of view.

- They look out for real people's needs and offer ways to fulfil them to appear kind. This means that they know even more than most top shrinks/psychologists etc. that humans have universal needs. How do they know this without training? In order to seduce people they will often offer to mow the lawn etc.

- Not all serial killers are psychopaths, some are multiple personalities – one of which is a 'malevolent alter.' The malevolent alter does the killing: the other personalities/alters may be unaware of its existence.

- The true study of psychopaths is known as 'Ponerology': 'the scientific study of evil.'

- Psychopaths seem to have almost 'telepathic' powers of rapidly identifying people's hopes and fears: they can work people out seemingly instantaneously. This itself would give them amazing powers of 'pseudo-rapport.'

- Their nature is destructive unlike real humans' which is creative. However a minority of psychopaths are very 'creative' but their 'art' is warped and deeply disturbed. It is cold, cruel, clinical and devoid of beauty.

- Christian Grey of 50 Shades fame has many classic psychopathic traits.

Psychopathic hypnotic seduction.

'The psychopathic bond.'

Research on their former victims has shown conclusively that psychopaths do sometimes rely upon hypnotic techniques to seduce and ultimately control their victims:

- They make use of – repetition.

- A mesmerizing tone of voice.

- Inducing a total focus on them and the relationship with them.

- Focused eye contact. (This is much more intense that real human eye contact.)

- The power of suggestion.

Psychopaths are essentially 'social predators' – with an animal instinct for precisely who will be prone, vulnerable, able to be 'taken in' (notice the languaging) to their suggestions. In a way like a stage hypnotist selecting the most suggestible subjects before a show, this is how and why these monsters in human skin are also inborn evil hypnotists.

Psychopaths brainwash their victims with a nearly **total focus on them** and on the relationship with them by **isolating them** from others. See the section on cults.

Ok, 2 immediate principles of hypnotic influence – fixation of attention, sensory deprivation, *therefore the essential need for human contact, acceptance and intimacy can only be met through the psychopath.* Psychopaths will discourage victims from other activities, they will monitor and monopolizing their time.

They use mesmerizing techniques such as...

- Staring into their target's eyes; women are especially susceptible to the power of strong eye contact which they see as attractive.

- Speaking softly and repetitively. Hypnotic cadence and brainwashing through repetition.

- They shamelessly use the power of suggestion to make victims fulfil their own psychopathic goals.

- The intent of psychopathic hypnosis is to control, manipulate and harm the victim, often also leading them to harm others in turn.

One victim admitted that her ex-boyfriend, a psychopath was superb at 'drawing me in' with seduction through his *voice.* She honestly stated, 'He had an incredibly sexy baritone voice,' which she admitted to the present day STILL HEARING IN HER MIND: he had installed his voice in her. ***Seduction hypnotists teach men how to do this on courses!***

The lady continued that through his 'tone and volume,' the monster created an '...instant hypnotic draw for me.' He had set up a series of re-induction triggers for her using his body language, eyes and 'the voice.' She further admitted she was so turned on by its voice that, '...it didn't take much to get me into bed.'

Sounds like a vampire in a horror film, like Dracula. The victim is manipulated to somehow invite in their own destruction. Truly powerful evil. How many women readers were honestly mesmerised and intrigued just by reading the above section???! Hmmm?

Women 'seduced' (seduction means to 'corrupt') into the psychopathic bond say the monster utilises flattery at first, then criticism (N.A.C: neuro-assocative-conditioning; see book 3, 'Powerful Hypnosis,' - push/pull - reward/punishment – like dog training) with the final aim of total domination, manipulation and control. See the section on cults for obvious parallels.

Victims/survivors of psychopaths think before their humanoid-monster encounter that 'abuse' (nominalised verb) means physical and little suspect the emotional, *sexual*, psychological and most importantly 'spiritual' element involved.

One (again) female victim of a psychopath reported that her ex-monster would speak to her in a dull monotone (on old time hypnotist trick) and she'd realise that she'd tranced out.

Interestingly many 'pick up artists' (P.U.A's) are simply teaching/selling psychopathic behaviour traits to men: again when normal people behave as psychopaths this is called 'secondary psychopathy.' This also occurs in psychopathically dominated societies known as 'pathocracies,' where psychopaths are seen as role models by real humans. Humans always look up the social totem pole to see how they should behave, what they should aspire to. Think Rome with their god worshipped emperors.

Women are attracted to men they perceive to be dangerous: fact. They often say 'I like him because he's a bastard,' – the 'bad boy.' There is a book about romance novels called 'Dangerous Men and Adventurous Women,' which explains the deep archetypal structure of women's 'romance' novels and why they will always have perennial appeal to the female psyche. *Fact: psychopaths have NO shortage of women interested in them, some women even marry them after they have been arrested. Psychopaths have no shortage of dates.* Ponder this.

Much evidence tells that psychopaths can spot potential victims from their vulnerable walk. They have an uncanny ability to spot women and men (there are female psychopaths remember, it's just male victims don't talk about things in the way women do) who were abused in childhood, thus rendering them more 'pre-conditioned' to be easily abused again. Some victims of psychopathic hypnosis have speculated that the more empathetic you are the easier you may be to hypnotise. This is probably true because empathy demands we imagine another person's point of view, feelings etc.

The hypnotic 'charm' of psychopaths.

Everyone who has encountered a psychopath talks about their 'charm' or as I call it c-harm/see-harm. What do we mean by charm and why is it SO hypnotic?

Let's look at some synonyms for charm; I have highlighted words which are most related to hypnotic powers:

Enchantment, allure, appeal, beauty*, **glamour***, grace, **magic**, agreeableness, allurement, attraction, attractiveness, **spell**, **witchery**, delightfulness, 'something,' star quality*, **bewitchery**, chemistry, conjuration, desirability, **fascination**, lure, **magnetism**, pizzazz, **sorcery.**

Words with a * next to them also denote
words connected with celebrity, fame.

We have connotations of magic. Of powerful
sex appeal. Of a 'drawing in' quality. Of
something indefinable that most others don't
have (because they are not psychopathic
monsters!). Let's delve deeper.

Word history.

The great American historian Will Durant
wrote that, '...he who knows the history of
words knows history.' Underlined words etc.
are those which relate to hypnosis.

- Charm: 1300 A.D. - incantation, magic
  charm.

- Derivation = Old French 'charme' 1200
  A.D., meaning - magic charm, magic,
  spell, incantation, song, lamentation.

- From Latin 'carmen' (like the opera!) -
  song, verse, enchantment, religious
  formula'; from 'canere' (canary) - to
  sing, to chant. The connotation is of

chanting or reciting verses of magical power.

- `A yet stronger power than that of herb or stone lies in the **spoken word**, (my emphasis) and all nations use it both for blessing and cursing. But these, to be effective, must be choice, well-knit, **rhythmic words** must have **lilt and tune**; hence all that is strong in the speech wielded by priest, physician, **magician**, is allied to the forms of **poetry**.´

Jacob Grimm, `Teutonic Mythology' 1883.

See my 2nd book, `Mastering hypnotic language,' for a full explanation of the above-mentioned principles.

- Charm: in the sense of `pleasing quality' evolved from 1700 A.D. onwards.

- Charm: meaning - **small trinket fastened to a watch-chain**, (think of the ye olde hypnotist's watch!!!!) etc.; first recorded 1865.

- Quantum physics sense is from 1964.

- To 'work like a charm' is recorded by 1824.

Additional meanings: from 1300 - to **recite or cast a magic spell**, from Old French 'charmer' - to enchant, to fill (someone) with desire (for something); to **protect, cure, treat**; to *maltreat, harm.* (My emphasis added.)

From Late Latin – 'carminare,' from Latin Carmen.

In Old French used alike of magical and non-magical activity.

In English, 'to win over by treating pleasingly, delight.'

From mid-1500s – 'Charmed; charming.' Charmed (short for, 'I am charmed,') as a conventional reply to a greeting or meeting is first recorded in 1825.

Nearly there folks!!! Charm is connected to...

'Delight.'

From 1200 A.D. – 'delit,' from Old French - delit = pleasure, delight, sexual desire. From 'delitier' - please greatly, charm.

From Latin 'delectare' (delectable) - to allure, delight, charm, please.

From 'delicere' (delicious) – to entice. Spelled 'delite' until 1600s, when it changed under influence of light, flight.

Finally! Originally a charm was a spell, literally **words of an incantation.** Then it came to mean an amulet or something worn on the person to ward off evil. From there it became a pretty trinket. It is also an attribute that exerts a **fascinating** or *attractive influence, exciting love or admiration.* It is a fascinating quality; charmingness. Charming means fascinating; **highly pleasing or delightful to the mind or senses.**

The psychopath's charm is said by victims to be like a spell, one that is so very hard to break. *It's been called a charm that 'relaxes defences, allays fear, paralyzes the mind, and induces trance.'*

This explains the 'spellbinding' hypnotic charm

of the psychopath.

On an NLP course when I was first learning this stuff, I pointed out to the trainer that psychopaths would LOVE this sort of information (psychos love learning 'methods of influence'). This made him VERY uncomfortable. He glowered at me when he thought I wasn't looking. Peripheral vision folks. I was right.

The hypnotic honeymoon with Dracula.

Some researchers of psychopaths say that hypnosis and trance are the, 'attraction heat, attachment magnet and bonding glue' of the pathological relationship.

They state that the monster is not just charming but superhumanly (non-humanly) incredibly charming. This 'charm' causes the usually female victim to **focus intensely** on him, as he **focuses intensely** on her. It is said to be **very pleasing to the mind and senses,** and it stuns your 'individual frontiers' and your instincts for self-preservation (think of the snake Kaa in the Disney version of the Jungle Book hypnotising Mowgli). It induces an engaging 'psychopathic trance' — where suggestibility is inevitable. Women admit finding themselves highly, compulsively desiring being the **focus** of his insidious powers again. They claim his 'winning smile' and intense eye contact captivate (to become a captive/imprisoned but 'willingly') them...**This super-charged charm is the first overt danger signal and it is addictive.**

Again inducing hypnosis comes naturally to the psychopath; they hypnotise their prey **repeatedly** and so become an anchor for that state on sight over time. When a victim intensely focuses on the usually breath-taking, jolting, startling, dynamic and enticing, witty, thrilling psychopath, she is aroused in more ways than one, she is repeatedly rewarded (at first), and motivated (dopamine release) to repeat such encounters. Psychos are glib and easy conversationalists. There is a reoccurring quality in victims' statements of a deluded 'too good to be true' and he's all mine mentality!!! Psychopaths have a natural yet unnatural intensity to easily gain and keep her ravished attention. *It has been described as an* *effortless soothing into a state of fascination where reality begins to vanish into oblivion:* this is what the seduction and honeymoon phase are all about. A good film to watch about this is the classic, 'A company of wolves,' directed by Neil Jordan.

During periods of hypnosis, the psychopath gives commands disguised as statements that use **symbolic language: *I have written in all 3 of my previous books about the power of symbols to implant themselves in the human mind because they are the language of the unconscious, especially for women who can access this part in waking states.*** Recent studies have shown massive cross-over activity in women between both hemispheres whereas men's brain's work back and forth on the same side. Psychos say stuff like...

'We have a very strong impassioned bond.'

Imagine this is said when the victim is in trance with a downward intonation – it becomes a command. It is also mechanical and clichéd although appearing poetic.

'I have you sealed in my heart.' (That's an order and a faux 'romantic' truism!)

In an interview I watched with a paedophile psychopath he used hypnotic tonality and embedded commands. As he spoke he would now and again...slow...right...down...his speech. But only in five second or so bursts; then he'd carry on as normal. At one point as he did this, he gazed deeply at the interviewer and said intensely –

'Trust me.'

While he seemed to be talking about something else.

Men teaching hypnotic seduction courses teach you how to use the symbolic language of women's unconscious minds!!!

These to me, inane phrases are operated upon in a powerfully influential way in the hypnotic trance state becoming deeply embedded and programmed into the victim's unconscious mind where they inveigle their way into conscious perception and alter it dramatically; precisely due to the emotional reality that they were absorbed within: a framework of intense bliss and ecstasy, hyper erotic/sexual connection, new couple bonding states and that honeymoon phase giddy-delight. This is pure state dependent learning. When the mind is emotionally aroused with pain or pleasure – you become programmable! Psychopaths just know this! *No normal human is born knowing this stuff.* Are psychos born or made? Hmmm? Good question.

Hypnotically 'playful' psychopaths?

To robustly strengthen the trance state the psychopath finds many avenues to induce it – so the state dependent learning becomes experientially total. Play, (apparently psychos are great fun to be around if you're that way inclined) flow, absorption: a cat always plays with a mouse before devouring it! So-called 'peak experiences,' such as sex, dancing etc. - when a heightened concentration creates that state women crave: 'that special connection.'

Female victims describe this hypnotic state as being highly addictive, dreamlike, as if reality doesn't exist and *you don't want it to.* Psychopaths exert a powerful drug-like intoxicating hold on these poor souls – the 'bond' is a monstrous parody of human love: a futile attempt at escape from the trials and tribulations of a harsh, cold, unyielding reality.

Some women report that when with the psycho-monster they felt totally 'wrapped up' – some use the metaphor of being in a 'bubble.' Some seduction gurus teach their clients to imagine that they have a golden bubble around them and the woman they are seducing!!! They also use metaphors of the voice 'wrapping itself around you.'

The good feelings the monster induces fade over time – the drug use law of diminishing returns. The unreality swiftly becomes a nightmare but the dopamine soaked memories of the 'good times' hypnotically draw the real human back for more. Part of the cause of drug addiction is that the 'junkie' visualises the hoped for wonderful consequences of using the drug. But the sad truth is that satisfaction can *never* occur. People whose universal human needs are not met are MOST susceptible to psychopath addiction. See my third book, 'Powerful hypnosis.'

Women also report feeling time distortion around these monsters: a sure sign of hypnosis. The conscious mind is often screaming danger but the addicted part, often referred to by women as 'the heart' is entranced and locked in. What they mean by the heart are the non-thinking parts of the brain – the unconscious.

The animalistic look.

'Predatory, animalistic, being eaten' – are just a few things said about the piercing hypnotic gaze of the monster. They will scan a woman's body up and down – not strong male sexuality oh no – like the terminator he is assessing you, your strengths your weaknesses. They also invade body space – this will grab your attention. Make you uncomfortable and seek 'rebalance,' almost a body language 'apposition of opposites.' Unbalancing a person makes them suggestible.

The psychos face is blank, seemingly he is 'cool' – no he is an emotionless monster. A psychologist who wrote a book about psychopaths said in a radio interview that when he showed a film of one of these beasts to his class ALL the girls wanted to date him because he looked 'cool.' O-k!

Without being taught how psycho-monsters use pacing, rapport, mirroring, seduction hypnosis, hypnotic commands, 'sleight of mouth' (suggestion/innuendo etc.), expressions, subliminal arousal techniques, and sensual domination as well as their innate unnatural allure. These things and more are all used by the psychopath to induce trance, hypnosis and suggestibility to subjugate their prey.

TIP 1: if you suspect a psycho avert eye contact. Think how Christopher Lee's Dracula would lock a victim's eyes on his before biting their necks!

Monsters are 'utilitarian' they see others as a means to solely material ends: their own. Sex, power etc. Assessment, manipulate/destroy, abandon are their modus operandi.

How psychopaths gain hypnotic rapport: The masks of evil.

- Your 'persona,' (social mask) lets a psychopath know which qualities you value in yourself. This mask may also give away the perceived insecurities/weaknesses you wish to conceal. Psychopaths are instinctive masters of studying Man and will then gently probe the person, testing for strengths, foibles, needs that are part of your deepest hidden and TRUE self. Now they can begin to tailor a relationship just for YOU. You feel he is a great listener: he is; he wants to know everything he can about you. A military attack analysis is occurring. He is sucking in everything he can to USE it against you at the right time. He 'love bombs' you: he gives you so much attention knowing most people need it and don't get enough, especially the vulnerable. Psychos look for needy people. It is like signing a pact with the devil – they offer to fulfil those needs at a price! This is their reason for 'living': for the monster he feels bored without it.

- Psychopaths compartmentalise thoughts into packages and display this through hand gestures. Look for dramatic hand movements (fixate and overwhelm attention) and 'props' – nonverbal mannerisms and gimmicks.

- They are wolves in sheep's clothing. 'What big eyes you have grandmother!' 'All the better to see you with!' said the wolf. 'What big teeth you have grandmother!' 'All the better to...Here ends Padawan our fascinating, short and chilling study of the hypnotic power of psychopaths.

A great starting place to study these fiends is **'Political Ponerology' by Andrew M. Lobaczewski** and **'Narcissism: denial of the true self' by Alexander Lowen.**

The way to 'cure' some skin problems using hypnosis.

Ok, now some skin problems are helped by using hypnosis: especially if the skin problem was originally caused by a stressor. I had a woman call telling me she had a 'dry skin' problem that had arisen ever since her husband's mum had died. After her death he had become more withdrawn. The lady's needs for emotional intimacy were not being met anymore. She went so far as to believe this threatened the future stability of her family. Her actual problem was an incredibly domineering and 'Nazi-like' mother who told her what to do and what not to do into adulthood! The end result was anxiety – the excessive worry and stress which had stemmed from her witch mother had gone into overdrive once her husband became distant in his prolonged grief. The point is you 'treat' the anxiety and the 'skin problem' will lessen or go away without any direct suggestions for skin healing. Emotional disturbances often reveal themselves in skin 'breakouts.'

Think how some people flush around the neck

when stressed, or when sexually aroused as womens' upper chests do. Blushing from embarrassment or coyness is another example. When some people cry, their face becomes bright red. *It's the stress chemicals that are doing it.* Even acne can be made worse by stress, anger, anxiety and fear.

There are known cases where some people had experienced guilt after surviving some kind of accident who later went on to develop skin problems as a result. I had a client who as a young child witnessed her father pretending to hang himself – she broke out in full-bodied hives. A friend developed hives when his sister divorced her first husband. If you can calm someone down in hypnosis and deal with removing unnecessary guilt or 'trauma' the skin condition can clear without medication.

Honestly with some skin conditions, even seemingly untreatable ones old time hypnotists have simply said,

'Your leg, arm etc. will clear,' repeatedly in hypnosis and it did. Weirdness!

The Rogue Hypnotist

For acne sufferers you can give suggestions to avoid picking spots, face touching, to change bedding regularly, to eat well, exercise, stop smoking/drinking: all of which have been proven to worsen the condition. You can even hypnotically train them to sleep on their back so the friction of resting on either side of the face cannot cause night-time outbreaks. These things won't work for everyone but have been known to help some. Basically hypnosis can reinforce desired behaviour modifications.

The client's self-worth has probably taken a bashing from the skin problem too, so it might be wise to give that a boost. Remember all skin condition affect self-image/confidence/esteem and can lead to extreme self-consciousness (going inside and 'imagining' what everyone thinks about you – a pathological trance); hypnosis can help with this ensuring a better chance of healing through reduced emotional stress/arousal. Stress and anger management can greatly improve existing skin conditions. Chronic skin problems are caused by internal and external 'stress' discuss...

The definition of waking hypnosis is?

Simply: a state of ***open-eyed*** hypnosis in which no ***obvious*** or formal trance induction is utilised. You can literally just do ANY hypnosis induction and leave out the 'close your eyes' instruction and get hypnosis with eyes open. Examples:

Reading a book: one that absorbs you utterly.

Driving a car: at the times when you trance out and your subconscious drives. Some say it is better than driving than the conscious mind anyway.

TV!!!: Nuff said.

An attractive 'other': person, object (jewellery/clothes/that new kitchen for women/cars for men); these can be elicited at supermarkets/shopping malls/online! Who knows anyone who goes into a buying state where they just can't stop buying useless s**t!? No of course you don't...

Live role play: 'Gamers' as they are called in the US; Warhammer, Dungeons and dragons all require waking trance and a good imagination. Historical re-enactment is an example too.

Ponzi schemes: any kind of illusory get rich quick con: such as any kind of lottery induces powerful waking hypnosis. You are more likely to be struck by green lightning several times.

Fashion trance: ok have you heard of the Teletubbies? Love them or hate them you know OF them right? Ok, so have you heard of a 'onesie'? This is quite simply a giant babygrow (US - onepieces) for adults. That's right adults are wearing babygrows/onepieces in the UK. They are regarded as the height of fashion at time of writing. *You can get people to do anything when they are culturally hypnotised. ANY F***ING THING!*

The Internet: powerfully hypnotic; at its worst it is a form of audio-electrical amphetamine. Online shopping addiction etc. is very real, I have treated it. There is significant evidence that the Internet is literally rewiring people's brains.

Computer games: when the person playing

these things **become absorbed** in the imaginary world of the game, they don't want to come out, they ignore all outside noises including other people talking to them. Anyone who has a little boy has seen that 'locked in' look they get while playing those games they love so much. It constitutes an extremely powerful state of waking hypnosis.

Magic shows: magic shows produce powerful altered states inherently; we know it's all a trick and we love trying to work out the riddle: our truth seeking template is activated. I was in a pub near Sloane Square in London and a street magician came up to me and 'put a cigarette' through my hand. I have no idea how he did it to this day!!! Mazing!

Cultural hypnosis: is waking hypnosis. See book 3.

Personalising N.A.C – the point to self, association trigger.

Ok, this is how you do it: say you want someone, anyone, prospective employer, potential girlfriend (it will be boys mostly interested in this, trust me) etc. to link nice qualities to you. Let's pick some nominalised qualities:

Trustworthy.

Generous.

Successful.

Intelligent.

Charming.

Now put these words into your speech anywhere. As you say such words simply point to yourself. The person's subconscious will pick up on the non-verbal physical embed that YOU have these qualities. Now if anyone tries this trick on you, you'll spot it. The reason people read so many books on influence is obvious: their human need for control and influence is not being met to any appreciable degree. Why else would you bother? There are better ways than 'casting spells' boys: far better ways.

Instant hypnosis: the 'hypno-pill.'

Old time hypnotists would pretend they had 'hypno-pills' (sodium pentothal etc.). These were truth pills that supposedly induced 'hypnosis' instantly if you took them. They were actually harmless sugar pills but when MOST 'patients' took them and were told, 'That's it. You become instantly more sleepy and tired etc.,' they went out like a light! It was the **belief** alone that did it.

Now modern clients will not take a 'hypno-pill,' it won't happen, I joked at the beginning about M and M's: but you could do this...

Hypno pill induction/deepener.

(With a highly hypnotically talented subject you may be able to induce trance with this alone from the waking state. Otherwise use it as a quick deepener. If you read book 1, 'How to hypnotise anyone,' start your induction and watch your client experience 'the moment of hypnotic surrender' and then instantly hit them with this; they are highly suggestible at this point of surrender)

'Imagine you have a hypno-pill in your hand...

Maybe you've taken a sleeping pill or know someone who did?

Maybe you just nodded off instantly on a car ride/train journey?

So, now, when I give you the hypnotic verbal signal...

imagine you swallow that imaginary hypno-pill and when you do...

you will instantly **go all the way down into deep hypnosis** *feeling blissful.*

Ready?

Ok...

SLEEP!!!! (The signal boys and girls)

Sleepier and more and more drowsy...

so tired...so...sleepy,

more and more tired...and so (yawn) sleepy...

so you just **NOD OFF!**

(It could work *spectacularly* with some

people; try it.)

In what environments is spontaneous waking hypnosis most likely?

Everywhere potentially but...

Exposure to advertising.

TV commercials, adverts at a sporting venue, adverts at a bus stop/shopping centre/on a train. The weirder, more 'eye-catching' the better. Evokes emotional states and issues commands. Even and especially charities do this: they are trying to elicit the emoto-state of guilt like...

Religious buildings.

I am not anti-religion but facts are facts: all major religions use costumes, spatial differentials between flock and 'priest' etc. Liverpool Cathedral in northern England instills 'Cathedral awe' in visitors, an altered state. The study of buildings and their psychological affect is known as architectonics. Religions use symbols, ritual, chanting, song etc. All hypnotic folks. Religious songs instill the required beliefs through mnemonics (easily remembered tunes etc.), repetition, words and acoustics.

In many religions 'holy men' wear black, a colour associated with oblivion, power and death! If you can be made to feel unnecessarily **guilty** you are controllable. Doesn't mean genuine guilt isn't a good thing.

Political election campaigns.

In the UK these are seemingly quite tame affairs but they are not. In the US they are very sophisticated forms of propaganda that seek to elicit emoto-hypnotic states in people through demonisation (name calling) campaigns. Due to the perennial law of diminishing returns they MUST get more extreme over time. I will cover P.R. and how crowds are hypnotically influenced in book 5, 'Wizards of trance.'

Doctors' and Dentists' offices.

Doctors often have no idea how suggestible 'patients' are. Or maybe they do and don't care. Saying 'you're x' (cancer/disease etc.) which means it's a part of YOU, instead of 'that x' which is dissociative is just one example.

Schools.

'When I blow the whistle stand still!' 'You're useless at maths boy!' (A global statement, usually a reflection of poor teaching.) Turning up at the school gates is a post hypnotic command to act as that 'social alter' called 'a pupil' or 'student.' It is these socially acceptable role changes that create 'ego states.'

Teenage 'rebellion' is the same as when the Romans allowed their slaves to pretend they were in charge for one day – to let off steam before the economic sledgehammer of the working world hits them like a ton of bricks.

Talking of which, schools main job is to train you for manager/labour relations in...

The workplace.

Does your boss tell you what to do? Do you do it? They have the power to make you homeless, starve you and your kids, make your life joyful or hellish. Bosses have far too much control over other people and it gives them MASSIVE waking hypnotic power. ***Most people cannot handle power.*** The King

Frodo; take off the Ring!

Home.

'Take out the trash, wash the dishes, do your homework,' said in a low, quiet or energetic (depending on circumstances) and 'serious' hypnotic tone. Mum/mom and dad are your hypnotists till you move out, and for some beyond that; unless you can think for yourself.

A therapist's office/home.

Not just hypnotists – ALL therapists put clients/patients into situational hypnoidal states.

A stage hypnotist show.

Self-explanatory I hope.

The Military.

Following orders, marching, killing. Marching is a rhythmic, mindless activity performed in a group (group hypnosis) in which you become suggestible. This is one reason why armies do it. It is also an efficient way to use energy to march in a particular rhythm. Eventually soldiers obey **without thinking:** waking hypnosis. If the critical faculty is down, that's waking hypnosis for a good cause or not mister! Soldiers make good hypnotic subjects as I said earlier.

Thinking, especially critical thinking is certainly NOT required of soldiers further than marshalling inner resources sufficient to fulfil orders within the military's hierarchical 'pyramid.' If you can enter a 'kill zone' and kill others who have never harmed you or yours in any way, a situation which could realistically result in your being crippled, disfigured, potentially losing a limb or being left with severe PTSD then you are 100% in the thrall of waking hypnosis.

When Western Christendom began to collapse in men's minds it was swiftly replaced by the totalitarian 'spiritualism' of fascism and communism. Nature and men's brain abhor a vacuum. With the death of the 'religion of peace' the undead ideology of the Hellenic civilisation of Rome and Greece was revived by the fascists: war and the warrior man as the ultimate ideal.

'We are becoming – and shall so increasingly,

*because this is our desire – a military nation.
A militaristic nation, I will add since we are
not afraid of words. To complete this picture:
warlike – that is to say, endowed with an ever
higher degree with the virtues of obedience,
sacrifice and dedication to country.'*

Mussolini 24.8.1934 and

*'War alone brings all human energies to their
highest tension and sets a seal of nobility on
the peoples who have the virtue to face it.'*

**_(Notice the great use of nominalisations
and trance language in both quotes? See
book 2 and see book 3, 'Powerful
hypnosis' on political trance)_**

*Excerpt from Mussolini speech, Enciclopedia
Italiana vol xiv 1934.*

Of course this is not to condemn the 'just
war'; a good example being the English nation
under King Alfred versus the psychopathic war
hordes in the Viking wars.

Art galleries. Lots of highly suggestible
people with very little critical faculties
intensely concentrating on 'works of art.' If

you believe 'modern art' is good you are a somnambulist!

Musical concerts. Fans in states of worshipful adulation of their 'celeb-man-god' in a mass crowd, with a 'mass-mind' listening to powerfully emotional music. The band or lead singer represents the focal point of waking hypnosis. I hope to cover hypnotic music in greater detail in a later work.

An NLP/hypnosis training 'seminar.' (Not all, this book isn't.)

Nightclubs. Nightclubs are very interesting. They are sub Saharan African in origin. The dance styles in nightclubs are (primarily) in derivation African; they are very similar to African tribes 'possession' rituals. The heavy, pumping bass activates the sexual centres of the brain and activates the waist down regions of the body. It is dark. Young people with bursting hormones are dancing unnaturally close to strangers. At this age most teenagers sense of identity is weak – they copy those that are *perceived* as being the 'cool kids'; these are generally the ones from the broken homes (attention seekers) and the egotists. There are a few flashing lights in the darkness, strobe lighting induces a hypnotic state. The mass dancing crowd is hypnotised by the DJ's suggestions and promptings. *Mass suggestion is inevitable with 99% of the crowd because they are in a crowd.* Tip of the iceberg on that one. Basically the nightclub is deliberately constructed to facilitate sexual trance if you haven't taken the hint.

Like I said: everywhere!!! In fact when aren't you being hypnotised???!

Singing away our mood.

You ever noticed that people give their moods away by absent-minded singing? Just notice what little ditties the people around you are humming etc. It will reveal much; note also the lyrics they sing out loud, it often dramatically states their frame of mind. One of the ways the subconscious leaks the truth. How will you use this knowledge? I'll give a tip later...

How to conversationally create light waking hypnotic states.

Get people to remember or imagine something, see book 1.

'Remember a time when you xd.'

'Imagine a time when you'll x.'

X of course represents the desired state. Imagining something can have an even MORE powerful affect than remembering something, because whereas revivification is made up of what was, (and attitudes to memory can naturally 'reframe' over time) what may be is both more exciting and filled with an anticipation to make it so. Imagination is the place where memory is recombined into 'fantasy' – fantasy can be good or bad.

Ok you won't like this but it's true so who cares: most people, including 95% of YOU reading this are in waking hypnotic states for most of the day. Some people are never truly awake.

What factors elicit waking trance?

1. External focus.

2. Suggestion.

3. Process/trance language.

4. Embedded commands.

5. Carrying out ANY physical activity. Sport, sex, washing up, making tea/coffee, driving, artistic activities etc. Anything that naturally elicits 'zone' or 'flow' states.

I'll give you a script to elicit waking trance using these principles later on. After studying its core component parts you should be able to manufacture your own. If you've read my other books you have probably figured out how to do it already.

Seduction trances: seductive hypnosis exposed!

Can you hypnotise someone into having sex with you? Yes. There are countless courses out there for sexually/emotionally frustrated men and men who wish to be a 'Don Juan' with the ladies. The hypno-sex gurus often pitch their wares like this:

'I was a 400 pound loser with a face like a bulldog licking p**s off a stinging nettle; I was hopeless with the ladies. No woman would ever date me and they always ended up saying, 'Can we just be friends?' One day after another failed encounter with a cute chick in Hooters I decided enough was enough! I decided to learn hypnosis/NLP/witchcraft and voodoo to seduce/make them like me and have sex with me! My new problem is controlling all my bitch ho's! Now I want to teach you my methods for getting your rocks off honey! If your dream is to have a sex addicted harem of sluts, just click here and download my invincible system: it only costs - $/£2000!!!'

It's generally cheaper to buy a hooker, then

you are guaranteed sex at a reasonable price. But men flock to this stuff like flies to s...some smelly stuff. Why? Because it claims to offer men the fulfilment of a vital human need. Sex and relationships, attention, social kudos, possibly love and also – *POWER!* Ah! There's the rub! It also appeals to the fantasy of having very many sex partners. The men who buy this stuff tend to be 'nice,' nerdy, academic, computer programmer types, they often lack social skills generally, have woeful self-confidence and weak masculinity. They are ALL lonely. You see how hypnotic these products/courses are to such men?

These business men and women (that's what they are folks pure and simple – they often pose as 'therapists') create personas that appeal to the men looking for love even if they ain't aware of it such as – 'The big sister you never had who will tell you what women really think...' 'The ugly nerd who became a stud muffin.' 'The world's greatest pick up artist ever on earth!' 'The man who solved the scientific secrets of attraction,' etc. They all claim to have what is desired – *secrets*. Beware of those who claim to sell secrets!!!

Secrets are hypnotic! Just the mention of them grab and fixate your attention by activating your truth seeking and desire for influence templates which then seek completion! Although these self-proclaimed sex god gurus are not running actual cults, real cults will often offer the secret of success etc. to hook you before ensnaring you totally. You have been warned. By the way what I have just said doesn't mean what the pervnotists sell doesn't work. At least on some women. They'd have no customers if that was true.

All this to one side: how do you induce a sexual trance? An attraction trance? Easy, I'll show you how. Ladies can see what a man might try on them and men can use it as they see fit or not at all. It's your choice. These courses are right about 1 thing: **sexual attraction is not a fixed static concept in a woman's mind – it is fluid and open to adjustment no matter what any initial reaction was. It is fluid because a woman's mind is fluid.**

The structure of hypnotic seduction follows this formula:

1. Get woman's attention fixated on you. Some 'gurus' advise tarot cards, palmistry, magic tricks, being the 'party guy,' hand writing analysis – all hypnotic. I would advise all hypnotists to study hand writing analysis (which does have some genuine merit) and palm reading (only for its hypnotic languaging etc.) Think outside the box! Some twee academic hypnosis course won't teach you this but I think you will be a better hypnotist for knowing it.

2. Get the woman hypnotically relaxed and fascinated, feeling comfort and an intense emotional connection to you using trance language.

3. Get her feeling attraction and sexually arousal in your presence. A.k.a – sexual tension. You can tell if this is building when a woman coughs nervously or more explicitly when she rubs her glass up and down as though it is a man's favourite plaything.

4. You condition her over time to feel sexually excited and turned on by you.

Depending on several factors she may sleep with you that day or night: it may take several meetings.

5. She sexually surrenders to you in order to relieve the sexual tension you have created.

6. Note: hypnosis based seduction methodologies probably won't work in noisy nightclubs – you need a quite-ish place – so she can hear you and relax.

*Word origin of 'guru' – from Hindi guru 'teacher, priest,' from Sanskrit guru/s 'one to be honoured, teacher,' literally 'heavy, weighty,' from PIE (Proto-Indo-European) root 'gru' – related to Germanic word 'grave' (as in the place your body goes after death!!!).

Sexual ambiguities in music.

All modern popular music is more or less about love or sex. These songs often use obvious sexual ambiguities. 'Get into the groove...' from a song by Madonna in one of her incarnations. What groove do you suppose she meant? 'Pussy cat, pussy cat I love you!'...sings Tom Jones, later he talks about kissing your 'sweet little nose.' What part of a woman's intimate anatomy do you suppose he was singing about? Think about it folks. If you watch Tom singing the 'sweet little nose' part in front of a live audience of women they squeal with delight and look ecstatic, eyes rolling. That's sexual hypnosis through sexual ambiguity in songs. Remember, if you read my other books, songs loop in the subconscious and can programme-in behaviour. Also you get more of what you focus on.

How to identify if someone is trying to hypnotically seduce YOU!

To 'seduce' someone you have to elicit a sexual trance state one way or another. I have crafted my own 'seduction' scripts below: their aim is to illustrate what can be done and how it can be done. I have deliberately over-egged the pudding to teach you how language alone without formal hypnosis can put someone into a waking trance state. No formal hypnosis course will teach you this; but you should know it to at least protect yourself from undue seduction by an unattractive pig! It will also help your general hypnosis knowledge. I think one of the reasons I am so much better than other hypnotists is because when I was learning this stuff I researched more areas of application than them: bizarrely sexual hypnosis can teach you principles that you can use to help people in terms of language precision and eliciting pleasant states. In sports this is known as cross-over training.

It is not necessary to adopt a 'bedroom voice' to use the scripts. A casual matter of fact manner may be better. What you do with this knowledge is up to you! Be careful.

All the training scripts that follow use:

1. Vividly descriptive and sexually suggestive language.

2. They paint pictures in a woman's mind which lead to feelings.

3. They elicit women's

personalised processes for attraction. Lust etc., sometimes through questions alone that elicit emoto-trance.

4. They all utilise waking hypnosis and light, sexual/emotional daydream trance.

5. They are all conversational and don't sound too weird. They just sound a bit 'dirty' by and large.

Seduction trance 1: inducing total fascination.

(Notice this is a psychopath's stage 1 fascination process!)

'Well it's interesting how people can **go into a social trance** *we've all done it...*

you know those times when you are with a certain person

and you just **feel fascination**

as you talk to them

your **forget about everything else**

almost as though while they talk

you **relax deeply**

you **feel comfortable** *with this person*

and we **feel good** *around people like that, don't we?*

I remember a time I was listening to someone speak

about something really fascinating and

and it was as though

this voice is hypnotic *you know...*

and I just found it easy to

pay close attention

to this person

as if nothing else really mattered for a while...

because the sound of their voice was

somehow nice and soothing

some quality attracted me...

it made me

feel warm and tingly inside...now

I was able to **focus on this person fully**

and as they spoke in a way that was naturally captivating

I found it easy to

become effortlessly absorbed.

Do you have times when you **experience that?'**

Feeling fascination quick double bind.

'When you **feel fascinated** _by a person_

does it happen instantaneously

or do you need to **relax** _first_

and gradually you **become absorbed**

by what they are talking about?'

Feeling a deep connection with someone.

(Everyone men included want a special connection; this is how to conversationally establish one)

'Can you tell me if this is true (seduction victim's name).

I read in a magazine around my friend's house

that women need to really

feel an instantaneous connection

with a person they are eventually going to sleep with.

I was talking to a woman

and she told me that

her feeling of connection was a certain colour...

*and when she can **relax** and **become absorbed***

by someone she finds very attractive

she imagines that colour of connection (colour feelings pattern)

spreading all through her mind and body

in such a wonderful way that makes her

feel delight,

*ever **experience anything like that, now?'***

Imagining things vividly.

(This is how to captivate someone's imagination; a process in brainwashing, seduction, psychopathic trance etc.)

*'You know when you read and you **go into trance***

when reading?

*And you **imagine** all the things that the author describes vividly.*

Can you think of a book that captured your imagination completely?

*You could **visualise** what the characters looked like*

what the world they inhabited was like...

so for a while it became vividly real like that in your mind...

I think that's why 50 Shades of Gray was so popular

because for women

sex takes place in the mind first;

a woman won't sleep with a man

*until she **pictures herself** and this other person*

f**king/having sex/making love.

And that book was successful because

many women **have sexual fantasies**

that are unfulfilled

they are fearful

of what might be unleashed

inside

perhaps they might

feel uncontrollable feelings of lust

like that sexy character in the story (the lead woman in 50 Shades is a drip but...)

who they identify with...

and as they read about her sexual adventures

vividly, excitingly be-coming realised
('coming' – sexual ambiguity)

a woman can **become absorbed in a sexual trance**

and as her mind drifts

she imagines what that man in that book

Is doing to that woman

is being done to her (bad grammar = hypnotic confusion)

and although she can **relax** *as*

she reads, she can also

feel that sexual tension building inside...

and I know that when

a woman enters that state, now,

in her mind

she imagines things

and that creates certain feelings

that can

really make her **feel deliciously hot inside.'** (When women are sexually aroused they feel warmth building.)

Sexy visualisation.

(Imagining sex is essential before sex takes place)

'When you read a dirty novel how soon does it take you to

relax into the imaginary world of the words *of the author*

so you can feel safe

*to **be so turned on***

by all the erotic things you imagine happening...inside?'

Feeling attraction script.

(Note: attraction is always best and much more flattering and ego-boosting when it just occurs naturally because it means someone sees something in YOU and not your words: 'attraction states' – state and therefore behavioural processes can be elicited through languaging alone)

*'We've all had times when we **feel very attracted** to someone haven't we?*

*And it's not like we have a choice to **feel those feelings*** *they just happen because attraction is not a choice...*

We are sitting there/standing there

and this person enters our field of view

we may not have ever seen them and BOOM!

You **feel intense attraction instantaneously...**

Some women tell me they get a unique set of feelings when they

see a man who attracts them deeply...

some say they **get tingles,**

a <u>prick</u>*ling sensation...*

Some say they **feel naughtily nervous...**

Others still say, **'You feel butterflies.'**

But I noticed that you **feel more attraction**

when they are attracted to you too...

this mutual attraction feeds off the other's attraction...

so not only do you think

'this man is attractive!'

but you also think

I **feel attractive**

and so

you **feel wonderfully feminine.**

Because in my experience

a woman likes a man

who makes her

feel very sexy, now...

You ever **have that happen?'**

<u>*Unconditional love elicitation.*</u>

(A feeling of total acceptance by at least one person is essential to human well-being)

'Is there anyone in your life

or has there been someone

for whom you **feel unconditional love** *toward?*

I get that with my dog/cat/nephew/pet monkey Harry...

If unconditional love were a colour

what colour would be for you?

Where do you **feel that feeling** *most inside?*

Where is it located?

Because all feelings belong somewhere.

As you **feel those emotions and sensations of total unconditional acceptance...**

could you imagine that colour feeling

spreading all through you

and **you're feeling that only intensify**

as it gets brighter and brighter and brighter

filling you with those amazing feelings now.'

Feeling romantic trance.

('Romance' which literally means 'of the Romans' is tricky: it's one step away from being wimpy or as they say in the US 'a wussy' and must be handled with care. You can elicit the feeling of romance by describing it)

'Romance is a funny thing isn't it?

women say they want it but

if a man is soppy/wussy and 'romantic'

in real life she generally goes off him fast...

So what is real romance?

I feel that romance is something every woman wants to feel

it's almost indefinable

like when **you slide into trance**

but when **you feel romantic**

237

or that someone is romancing you...

I think it's a feeling women get

you know that feeling don't you?

Almost like **you're entering a romantic trance...now...**

It's not so much the flowers as the feeling in you they provoke...

What colour would that romantic feeling be?

Where does it start and where does it move to next?

What happens if that colour gets brighter?

Do **these romantic feelings only intensify?'**

(Note to hypnotist: notice you can elicit all states using colour feelings and symbols alone!)

That rude man.

(Erickson used his 'My friend John' pattern also known as the 'quotes' pattern – see book 2 – 'Mastering hypnotic language.' *You dissociate the smut your spout from your mouth by saying someone else said it,* the emotional/hypnotic effect is the same)

*'I can't **f**king** believe this!*

That man had huge balls saying it!

He just went up to this sexy woman,

looked her straight in the eye and said...

*could you **imagine me going down on you...***

*and you **feel so f**king fantastic***

*that it began to **drive you wild with desire...***

And as that warmth builds...

inside you...

*I bet you'd start **imagining me***

f**king you in all the ways you always secretly deeply desired!

Now, that takes lot of spunk!' (Me being

rather excessively smutty to make a point; sorry but we are grown-ups!)

The porn pre-sex induction.

(I got the idea for this by remembering a time - long ago - when I asked my best friend how to bring up the topic of sex with my very first proper girlfriend. He said, 'Just talk to her about sex...' With that in mind...)

'You know pornos are all the same...

after they **kiss and strip off...**

first this horny man goes down on this woman...

he's licking her ****y out and she starts moaning with desire...

you know, you've seen that right?

Next this woman starts s**king this man's big, rock hard c**k...

This woman is really into it...

All her mental focus is on this man's c**k...

Usually he's holding onto her head or gripping

her hair

and thrusting himself b**ls deep into her mouth...

and she loves this experience...

Can you **picture it vividly...**

Then he gets this woman and he starts

to suck her breasts and you can see

this woman **get so turned on** *as this man*

just licks her n*****s in the way she likes.

Fondles her soft b****ts in a way that makes her moan...

Soon **this man and woman f**k**
('this man' will be interpreted as the speaker)

he's thrusting himself into her p***y (a cat metaphor)

while he sucks her toes...

then he flings her over

and **can you imagine**

f**ks this woman d***y style... (A canine comparative)

she arches her back in delight

and he slaps her arse

and pulls her long hair (Maybe she's a 50 shades kinda girl??)

as his c**k penetrates her deeply... (No, not his cook)

etc...'

(Note: in real life if you are going to tell a woman what you want to do to her sexually and when that is appropriate and something *she'd like too* – do not be vague. They like it when you describe precisely what you want to do to them very vividly. If you haven't got the guts to be bold in description what use will you be in bed or potentially fathering her children? You can use this principle in naughty emails, text, phone sex, online chat. Not that I ever have – ahem!)

The surrender to seduction induction.

(Remember women want to sexually submit

to men they are sexually attracted to. Her nature is to be sexually submissive; this is the basis of eroticism.)

'You know in almost all animals before they mate

the female surrenders sexually to the male...

Women **want to be sexually dominated in bed**

that's the truth...

and lots of men don't even know that...

but we surrender in other ways too...

what things have you surrendered too?

What other things have you irresistibly surrendered to?

We've all had experiences like that, have we not?

It's like the conscious mind steps aside

and lets out all these unconscious feelings

that inevitably lead to surrender...

and that might be sexual surrender too...

it might be like when you

surrender to a seductive kiss

with a sexy stranger/a certain man...

what process do you go through inside

that lets you know

you want to sexually surrender to this man?'

(Some people, the sex hypnosis gurus, claim they invented this stuff in the 1990s – total B-S, they may have revived it but these sorts of techniques are ancient. Also Erickson used this type of language at least once with a female patient.)

The erotic food script.

(I am being silly, over the top and ludicrous to make a point and teach you how this is done in seduction hypnosis. It uses sexual metaphor: crudely yes, I'll grant you that!)

'You know I'm a hypnotist

It's really just about teaching people

*how to **use the imagination.***

*How to **access that part...now...***

Ever bite into a lemon?

It's so yellow and juicy looking,

most people even if they

don't like lemon

can picture slicing one open...

seeing all those juices flowing out...

imagine biting into that flesh...

*and they **have a reaction** as if it's real.*

So everyone likes ice cream...

I used to love this thing called Walnut Whips... (kinky!)

What was your favourite sweet as a child?

Well a Walnut Whip

was chocolate on the outside...

a sort of chocolate whirl that formed a peak...

just thinking about it makes my mouth salivate...

in anticipation...

if you can **see it**   (command to 'hallucinate')

this sensuous thing that built to a peak...

it had a big delicious nut on top of it...

You know the kind of fat juicy nuts

like brazil nuts,

that you really want to suck and taste in your mouth...

feeling all that *nut juice*

rolling around your tongue...

and if you bit the nut off

the top of that chocolate base

inside...

your tongue could <u>penetrate</u>

into this delicious, soft, warm and sticky

viscous white vanilla flavoured stuff...

I have no idea what it was called...

But you could **use your tongue**

to probe inside the tip of that thing

still tasting a bit of the nut juice...

as you swirl that tongue inside it

lapping up that <u>sticky white stuff</u>...

and sucking the tip of that chocolate whirl,

feeling that creamy texture

of the <u>hard and rigid</u> outer chocolate... (sexual ambiguities underlined)

and the inner sticky white stuff

and you just had to

wolf that delicious white stuff

down

all the way down...

inside your mouth

and feel it slide inside your throat

*in a way that made you **feel warm inside...'***

<u>*Summation.*</u>

I might cover this topic in more depth in a later book; so many outright loser/ weirdos are teaching 'perv-nosis' as I call it. Maybe I should teach you the ethical use of it??? We'll see. You can idea seed sexual themes by using sexual swear words, sexually ambiguous words, bawdy words and phrases etc. Remember sexual swear words are slightly shocking and produce mini suggestible states or 'micro trance loops.' We'll deal with this later.

How to speak process/trance language.

Process language is vague as I have said in my other books. I have given you lots of examples of how to use it in various scripts etc. We all use process language in everyday life – you have to, it saves time. The great writer C.S Lewis possibly believed woman had a natural tendency to do this by dropping nouns from speech. He claimed men would say stuff like,

'Place this dish inside the bigger dish which you'll find on top of the red shelf.'

Whereas woman would say,

'Put this in the other one up there.'

We all do it when we lie, try to cover things up or aren't really considering if what we've said is clear to anyone but ourselves. A method you can use to really master 'process talk' is to read very good hypnosis scripts which are full of it and analyse them and learn by osmosis. Or you can do the following: take any book, preferably a novel and turn the words (preferably texts with lots of specific words) into process words. I will do so below as an example by taking a random paragraph from Homer's Odyssey, the part when the witch Circe warns Odysseus of the dangers that face him and his crew. I take out all specific references and make them generalisations.

'After you have travelled past the monsters, many paths present themselves. You must take you own path without my assistance. One path is dangerous by threat of being dashed against the high rocks by giant waves. No flying animal, even those favoured by the chief god may pass that way. Boats always sink there; remnants of wood and many bodies show they fall victim to these waves and strange fire blasts too! Only one world famous boat has passed through as it headed home from foreign travels. If the most powerful goddess had not favoured the beloved hero who captained the boat by speeding it through, it too would have sunk.'

By doing this you almost make the text like a children's book. The language that the subconscious responds too is often more 'concrete' that is more 'childlike' than normal speech, though it can process all types of language. **As a good hypnotist you should be able to go into process speech at will.** *All process speech is hypnotic because it* **demands** *the listener 'fill in the gaps' with their own imagination – you can fractionate merely by switching repeatedly between specifics and generalities.* Remember from my other books that you can deepen trance each time you take someone in and out of it.

How to describe something vaguely to induce relaxation.

If someone imagines something it is perceived to be their thought and so more likely to be acted upon. This is the overwhelming power of creating mental images. To do so ask the following questions and then describe vaguely or in detail like a novelist if you prefer...

- What can you see?

- What can you hear?

- What can you smell?

- What can you taste?

- What can you feel inside?

- What can you touch?

Let's take for our example having a picnic in a wood.

What can we see?

'It's a nice sunny day. You're sitting in an open meadow lined with trees.'

(All detail left out, not oaks and elms – trees –

this is a variety of 'linguistic minimalism,' which is by and large not a good thing in real life – think 1984 Doublespeak etc.)

What can you hear?

'You can hear the sound of the summer breeze rustling through the leaves. The sound of cows mooing in the distance and the birdsong in the trees.'

What can you smell?

'You can smell the freshness of summer all around you. The scent of summer flowers. The smell of that drink you've brought with you. The smell of all the delights of that picnic laid out before you.'

What can you taste?

'You bite into that delicious sandwich. Taste those amazing flavours; let them roll over your tongue – it tastes wonderful!'

What can you feel inside?

'You feel utterly connected with nature, life and the world. You feel great just being alive on days like this. You feel a deep connected

joy! You feel that comforting feeling anyone gets after a good meal.'

What can you touch?

'After lunch you go for a walk and rub your hands along the rough bark of the trees as you once did as a child. Feel the breeze on the skin of your face. Your fingers feel the texture of certain leaves.'

Easy and this can be done while someone is wide awake, **they have to visualise it to understand it** and then – you will swiftly have them in light waking hypnosis.

If someone is wary about being hypnotised just say,

'Would you like me to show you how to really relax easily?'

Pretend hypnosis is just relaxation. You know better of course.

Phobic metaphorical removal.

This is a version of a story I heard quite a while back, sometime as I was starting to learn this nonsense about 20 years ago: it was my first **exposure** (sexual connotations!) to hypnotic metaphor. I call it 'The Emperor of the Gods'; I sometimes throw it in with anxiety, fear, phobias, panic etc. the message is I hope obvious.

The Emperor of the Gods.

'As a child we all had our favourite stories and our favourite story tellers. Once upon a time the Emperor of the gods decided to go on a trip and leave all the little gods in charge. While he was away a big monster came towards the castle they lived in and they grew very afraid; and the more scared they became the bigger it grew until it was gigantic. The little gods quivered and cowered behind the castle walls. Just at that moment the Emperor of the gods came home and saw what was happening...'Oh you fools!' he laughed. This is no monster, this is fear, he lives on your fear of fear. 'Oh!' said the little gods and as he did the monster began to shrink and shrink until it

was no bigger than a mouse. 'Shall we get rid of it?' asked one of the little gods. 'No' laughed the Emperor, 'Let's keep him, he might have some uses, sometimes, from time to time...'

How to condition a woman to orgasm on command without formal hypnosis.

I thought **long and hard** about whether I should include any 'perv-nosis' and thought: why the hell not! Ok now this is mainly for men and lesbians I suppose. Not really; I have included this 'unique' example of N.A.C to let you see just how widely 'hypnotists' apply their learnings. Clearly the 'sex obsessed' ones.

1. Have sex with your girlfriend, lover, wife etc. Bring her to orgasm.

2. At the peak of her orgasm say: *'Come for me baby! Come for me baby!'* Or something else similar.

3. For the next 20 times you make love and bring her to climax say your trigger phrase. Note also: when a woman's eyes roll back in her head showing the whites during lovemaking – she is psychologically pliant!

You have now established a powerful 'anchor' (N.A.C – Neuro-Associative-Conditioning; see book 3, 'Powerful hypnosis!') with her orgasm and your trigger phrase. As women are capable of psychological orgasm say your orgasm on cue phrase and see what happens. Preferably NOT in the local supermarket!

Why does this work? Because when your girlfriend/wife is in a heightened state of sexual arousal she is hypnotised: remember **LUSTNOSIS?** Ok, so she becomes highly suggestible in that state. As bugs bunny used to say: ain't I a stinker!

Whatever grabs your attention is potentially hypnotic.

If a woman wears a low cut dress and reveals her cleavage many men will be hypnotised – so hypnotised that they'll have trouble averting their eyes! The same with women who are hypnotised by a man's shiny, new car! Or wallet!

Notice that when an ambulance drives by most people stare after it like ghouls wanting blood and drama? Notice how loud bangs from back-firing cars, rogue fireworks etc. make everyone look?

A new film is released: everyone wants to see it – it has 'grabbed the popular imagination' as the saying sort of goes.

Look at someone who you've hypnotised before.

'Can you remember the last time you were hypnotised?'

As they go inside a little to recall this, instantly slap your hands together making a big CLAP noise and say in a commanding tone –

'SLEEP!'

And they may well go out like a light!

NOTE: leaders are the focal point of attention for a 'crowd'; what does that tell you?

Waking 'non-verbal' hypnosis.

What is this? A cough, an itch, a yawn, a swallow! If you can get someone to carry out these small unconscious behaviours you have achieved waking hypnosis.

- Just cough in a lift and see if someone copies you.

- Yawn in company and see if they follow suit. Or say, 'Isn't it funny how *yawning is infectious?'*

- To get an itch you can talk about when a flea was on you. Or just talk about creepy crawlies. Or you can say...'*My friend **nose**/knows he's right when he doesn't feel an uncomfortable '**itch'** anymore, if that makes sense?*

- To get a swallow response say...'*In a moment you will have an uncontrollable urge to swallow and it won't feel right till you do.'*

That's just to get you thinking. Why does it work? Because you are directing someone to things they do take notice of now and again anyway. We may need an itch half the day but are so busy doing other things we don't notice it. Until it's pointed out. But suggestion can create these sensations alone.

Why is a hypnosis teacher the teacher and you the student?

Because they've read more books on it than you. That's it. Read as much as you can on hypnosis – all books, old books especially (pre NLP influence), new books, not books by weirdos though. So many hypnotists are SO creepy and odd. Look at the books they sell – 'Use hypnosis to control others to do your bidding!' Life-get. Look at the face of the author if he has a picture: does he look weird? Does he boast a lot or go on about himself as some sort of genius/star etc. when no one has in fact heard of him? If so – run!

Behavioural change through waking hypnosis and implication.

We've all seen this one: boy walks up to girl way out of his perceived league. He is so desperate for her approval – 'If only *she* knew I existed everything would be fine!' He starts lamely asking her what music she likes. As if to at least feign interest she asks what music he likes. He replies,

'Blah (name of group).'

'You like *them*???!' she says. Not anymore he don't! Having a weak sense of who you are is no way to seduce a lady, that aside; what she did is a mild form of waking hypnosis through implication.

Some relatives bought my nephew an air hockey table; it was big so they decided to check with his mum, my sister if it was ok.

'Where am I going to put it?' she replied to their query. It went back to the shop.

You can use waking hypnotic implication to change behaviour by humorously implying that doing x is idiotic, unflattering, potentially unpopular/unfashionable, unworthy. My brother's godchildren were never really told off, their mum would just say,

'I can't believe you did that.'

Old time hypnotic powers revisited – improving 'traditional hypnosis':– modern pocket watch variation and analysis.

You can get women under your hypno-spell by using 'magic charms,' women can have their minds captivated by the promise of 'magic' and 'spiritualism.' This is well known.

Let's imagine an old time hypnotist and how he might just hypnotise a woman who has booked an appointment for 'incurable' x (the problem) in just 3 sentences. Perhaps she is very desperate and highly motivated to change. Let's also say he promises he will have his 'hypno-trinket' (the prop/plausible ritual) as she has seen someone hypnotised in a favourite movie using one. He is of course pacing her reality of what she believed was required to get hypnosis. To cut the story short she turns up excited the next morning, sees the trinket and declares, 'Oh just like in the movie!'

The spell could run thus...

'Very soon I'll count from 1-3...

and sway this pocket watch in front of you...

*and your **eyes** will **become very, very heavy***

as you watch that watch...

*and you will **fall into a deep hypnotic sleep, now.**'*

Tick, tock, tick, tock

1.....2....3...'

Line by line analysis.

'Very soon I'll count from 1-3...

(Not now but in a moment pattern – see book 2: guard goes down because nothing is happening now, subconscious primed to run automatic hypnosis template...also a statement of bland fact – a truism.)

and sway this pocket watch in front of you...

(Truism – you are swinging it, a concrete reality therefore not resisted, woman fixates attention on locket – narrow focus of attention.)

and your <u>eyes</u> will <u>become very, very heavy</u>

(Expectation already set as woman had seen film in which person was hypnotised this way – plus the first overt command/suggestion. 2 pacing statements and a 'lead' – a suggestion to manifest trance behaviour. Watching a dangling watch, a modern one held by one part of the wrist strap would work by the way, it will also tire the eyes helping as a convincer of 'falling to sleep' = again a concrete reality 'convincer.' Notice the coded embed – 'eyes – become heavy etc.')

as you watch the watch...

(Pacing statement – they are watching it, plus confusion/ambiguity + alliteration/assonance – 'watch the watch.')

and you will <u>fall into a deep hypnotic sleep.'</u>

('and' false linkage and compounding suggestion 'if you do x, y will follow' – no reason it should, merely 'trance logic' and expectation of client. Embed – 'fall into' etc. You don't have to use embeds, the oldies didn't but why not weigh things in your favour as the conscious mind is well and truly fixated on the watch?)

Tick, tock, tick, tock...1.....2....3...'

('Tick-tock' - age regression/rhythm, repetition –*mantra* - of word 'numbs' consciousness. Time the words/number with the swing to the right - *right hemisphere of brain associated with trance*. Woman's eyes fixated, unconscious prepares for trigger word '3' to trigger hypnosis response. Simple and highly effective. Expect deep hypnosis in about 15 seconds using this old fashioned method! Wow! I'd throw in a deepener to intensify things.)

You see how if you have read my other books you already know the principles of how to do this! There's no difference, the same mechanisms are at work. In this book I am seeking to prove with multiple sources that what I said in the first 3 books is true.

We see at least 9 hypnotic principles in those

4 short sentences and the build-up.

1. High motivation through desperation to change.

2. 'Opportunism' as some oldies termed it or 'utilisation' as Ericksonians call it.

3. Expectation and intent.

4. Fixation of attention/plausible ritual.

5. 'In a moment' pattern.

6. Truisms.

7. Pacing and leading.

8. Compounding suggestion/false linkage.

9. Trigger word.

Old style hypnosis didn't use much weird languaging if any but there was a simple and effective language work occuring. The words were direct. No embeds etc. That's the only difference really and it worked superbly. The oldies used props to fixate attention – a crystal ball, a whirling spiral, that kind of stuff; to give the illusion of it being a magic trick when it just relied on fixed and immutable patterns of mind. Props are like Dumbo's feather: he could fly all along.

The 'I – you' shift.

The so-called 'I-you' shift is an example of covert manipulation. If you want someone to experience a state, you simply talk about yourself experiencing it (the 'I' part). And at some moment of your choosing you switch to saying they are experiencing it (the 'you' bit.)

*'**I** was on holiday and driving this boat on the Norfolk Broads; **I** was surrounded by this flat, wide open space, **I** began to **feel so relaxed;** my mind was clear and at peace, the sky was yellowing and turning toward dusk. My only companions were the tall reed patches, the trees on the embankment and the occasional sound of the fenland birds; **you** could **feel an almost magical atmosphere**, as though **you** feel at one with nature...'*

See how easy and simple it is to do? A very subtle, almost imperceptible gear shift is involved.

How to do 'modern' prop hypnosis: again.

Modern version of pendulum gazing induction.

But can we moderns improve on the oldie but goodies stuff? Of course – we will add our new hypno-tactics to our arsenal. You have to pay for props...you could use a clock with big hands instead feasibly...or just get someone to close their eyes and imagine doing the following...it works equally well if not better!

Set up a pendulum or pendulum watch/metronome is fine. Get person to,

*'Just **fixate your attention** on that pendulum.*

(Staring/eye fixation is hypnotic.)

As you simply watch it swaying from side to side

(Truism and suggestion.)

*and **become fascinated, absorbed...***

(Embed.)

you'll **fall into a deep hypnotic sleep!'**

(...False link 'you'll' + embed.)

as you do, it will become very, very hard for you

(As you do = a re-inforcer suggestion and false linkage + suggestion 'it will be hard' etc.)

to move your eyes from side to side...

(a 'negative' is still processed – brain just thinks – 'Keep eyes still.')

And anyway...

(Conversational fluff. Fluff and waffle/redundancies can aid elicitation of hypnosis.)

you have only one wish...

(Internal narrow focus + age regression word 'wish.' You can use 'desire' but it has slight sexual connotations.)

that is to **fall into a deep sleep.**

(Pause for a few minutes while you let them do this...)

Focus your attention on the idea of
your/'re falling into a deep hypnotic trance...

(This means 'go inside' and ponder – giving consciousness a task to take it offline.)

*Only in your mind but on the out breath repeat the word **Sleep!***

(This self-talk occupies/distracts consciousness, self-hypnosis/meditation principle of repeating one thing – narrowing focus. Plus overload, very quickly the brain is being given multiple tasks – rapidly compounding suggestions.)

Sleep!

(In time with the pendulum/metronome. When meditating people say a word on the out breath; + an embed.)

Sleep!

With each swing of that pendulum...

which you are watching closely...

(Truism/command. If you want eyes open hypnosis – leave them open, or say...)

And your eyes can close as soon as you are ready...'

(Etc.)

How to avoid therapist burnout with inappropriate humour.

Why you should give your client's nicknames.

Folks I find it very therapeutic to give certain clients nicknames. Never tell them this, don't let them suspect this but do it. It makes the whole thing more fun and makes it more light-hearted for you! Naughty? Yes, just do it and notice how you take things a bit less seriously even if the problems they have are serious. It works.

Why you must watch 'What about Bob,' because you will meet him!

Watch the film comedy 'What about Bob,' starring Bill Murray and Richard Dreyfuss. If you are a therapist you will meet your 'Bob.' I have had three: these are the clients who keep coming back and driving you mad! In the film Bob (Murray) is actually saner than his shrink (Dreyfuss). Very funny film that will hopefully help you lighten up about working with the mentally troubled and avoid burnout.

Hello Seattle...I'm listening.

Frasier was a superb comedy about a loveable Harvard trained shrink/snob who first appeared in the great American sitcom Cheers. Never do what Frasier does, he's just like an agony aunt giving out advice but again it may give you the opportunity to lighten up about the whole mad, mad world of therapy. A laugh a day keeps the doctor away. That last piece of trite advice reminds me of Brian the Dog in Family Guy (who they just killed off but wisely brought back) who wrote a pathetic self-help book that became a best seller called, 'Wish it, want it, do it!' Is this my wish it, want it, do it????!

The apposition of opposites principle.

Although I very rarely use this in clinical practice it is best you learn it. The only time I knowingly use it is in the indirect command for amnesia –

'You can **forget** to **remember** what you **remember** to **forget**.'

This hypnotic principle works because it facilitates a split/division in consciousness – i.e. 'the hypnotic overload principle.' The mind only likes to do one thing at a time.

Some researchers into hypnosis have suggested this principle works as it emulates the entire nervous system's 'balance between opponent systems.' The apposition of opposites may well exploit this inbuilt bias. Who knows? Boffins do like to say things just for the sake of saying things. A theory is not reality.

Simple, double-bind examples are –

*'As you focus on the **tension** in that hand your leg can **relax**.'*

*'The more you TRY to **remember** the more*

*inevitably you **forget**.'*

*'Perhaps one part of you feels **heavy** as another part feels **lighter** somehow.'*

<u>*Notice they are all dualities of possible hypnotic phenomena.*</u> By emphasising one aspect ('directionalisation'/focus) of reality there instantly arises the natural, neurological tendency to do the opposite to maintain the lost equilibrium. By offering opposing suggestions swiftly you steer the neurology back to equilibrium – like unbalancing and rebalancing a person repetitively. You can also quickly compound suggestions and overload consciousness. This is similar to unbalancing someone physically which fires off the brain's 'orientation response,' which alerts us to any new stimulus that may need attention and for some reason temporarily stuns us. This is why acting training and sensitivity training (which are pretty much the same thing) use the 'trust fall' whereby you fall back into someone's arms without preparing to hit the ground. It makes you suggestible and begins to play with your sense of reality.

'A part of you (apart of you – dissociative)

*may feel **warm** as another part feels comfortably **cooler**.'*

*'When we focus on one part of us that is **hypersensitive** to touch another part may be quite unexpectedly **insensitive**.'*

These examples are all truisms. A slight variant of this principle is the 'more less' language pattern, which can on occasion linguistically approximates the formula -

'The more of x, the less of y.'

*'The more you pay attention to that **growing relaxation** spreading, the less that **old tension** bothers you before it melts completely.'*

*'The more you **listen to my voice** the **quieter** you can become inside.'*

*'The more you focus on your increasing hypnotic **confidence** the less unnecessary **doubts** will hold you back.'*

Erickson used this principle in therapy. When greeted by a client who believed dental work MUST be painful he hypnotised him to feel pain in his hand and not his mouth which remained quite numb. Interestingly this mirrors a principle of Greek Rhetoric illustrated here in an excerpt from a quote from former US President Abraham Lincoln.

'...with public sentiment nothing can **fail**; without it, nothing can **succeed**.'

Such ancient tricks successfully exploit the 'aural prejudices' of the human ear. I will cover them in more depth in book 5, 'Wizards of trance,' in which we will cover many 'influence technologies' in far greater detail.

There are much more complex ways to use this in hypnotherapy. Some hypnotherapists prefer to connect an action of the body to an action of the mind: that is, psychological change...

*'As that hand still holds that **anger** won't it be nice to know that that mind can **calm** down.'*

<u>*To practise the creation of apposition of opposites pick two opposing principles and link them in one suggestion.*</u> Write down about 5 – 10 varieties to wire them in.

Mass waking hypnosis extraordinaire: The Father Christmas conspiracy!

One of the greatest acts of mass waking hypnosis in the West is what I have light-heartedly termed, *'The Father Christmas conspiracy!'* This is where ALL grownups tell a complete and bare-faced lie that a benevolent bearded house breaker drops presents down the chimney (who even has a proper chimney anymore!?) if children are very, very good! This represents a wonderful hypnotic reality that little children fall for hook, line and sinker! It is a great tool for behaviour modification too! We buy trees, decorations, mouth-wateringly tasty food; the reality of which only convinces our tiddlers that it's all real!

The reality of St.Nick's origins lie in the Scandanavian god 'The Winterman,' a fearsome strawberry-skinned giant who bore a tree club and was accompanied by a devil-looking accomplice called Skopje, who would suck out the brains of naughty children! We have thankfully 'Disneyfied' the myth and made it much more charming. Into their little heads we pour a delightful delusion that even scares them a bit, at first,

'How will he get in the house!!?' they worriedly ask.

This is a pure case of ***believed in imaginings*** which was an explanation of what hypnosis was by psychiatrists Crasilnick and Hall. Of course there are many, many more odd and dangerous delusions floating around, infecting brains, and Father Christmas at least is fun! Fantasy is good for us by the way – J.R.R Tolkien called it the 'secondary reality.' Just be sure it's your fantasy or if it's someone else's keep your critical guard up until you KNOW their values are similar to yours. Acting as though something is true when it isn't is waking hypnosis.

The psycholinguistics of sexual ambiguities for flirting, sales and 'power.'

You may fairly ask why study this while learning about hypnosis? Because you should know ALL applications of this stuff that's why. If you are just looking out for linguistic manipulation in one area of life or suspect it's not used in another you'll have a blind spot. **Sex is an important part of adult life, fact. In fact sex, its gratification and withholding is used to control men.** Do you think some NLPers and hypnotists are NOT going to use their knowledge to get laid? Of course they are. After I expose some of their tricks you'll be able to detect it and thwart it or go along with it; but the important things is – *you'll have the choice.* The way these men justify their actions is often along these lines...

'I am not very good looking; this places me at a disadvantage when trying to get the 'best looking' women to have sex with. I don't have a big car or house, I'm not financially successful. Why should all the a**holes get the best women etc.? BUT I know what <u>words</u>

to use to turn a woman on!'

Whatever ultimately anyone thinks of the rights or wrongs of this form of waking hypnosis – let's study it 'scientifically.' I guarantee that you'll be a better hypnotist by doing so. _You'll also find cross over areas where the principles behind it can be used in other areas of life, even therapy._ I think its fine to use double-entendres when flirting. We can't all live like nuns in a convent can we! It's funnier and wittier and naughtier than using somewhat creepy 'seductions scripts.' These things are best when they happen spontaneously. Ok let's delve into the bawdy world of words...

Conversational smut.

F**k me that's not true!

Screw it!

That man is a **big c**k!**

What a pair of **t*ts** those idiots were.

You are such a **wet p***y!**

Come inside!

Swallow it back!

That was a **titillating** experience.

Suck my big fat hairy ones!

And in high art.

Mercutio's line from William Shakespeare's Romeo and Juliet,

*'Tis no less a good day, I tell you; for the bawdy hand of the dial is now upon the **prick** of noon.*

If it's good enough for big Will folks. Ooops!

Charles Dickens' character in Oliver Twist named Charley Bates but frequently referred to as 'Master Bates.'

Charles **Dick**-ens. Hmmm?

The James Bond character 'Pussy Galore' in Goldfinger. Flemming just liked cats???!

There is a Belamy Brother's song, 'If I said you had a beautiful body, would you hold it against me?

From The Simpsons; Marge is due to board a

ship to Skull Island, Smithers says 'I think women and seamen don't mix.'

Another Simpson's episode, Kent Brockman declares as gold is discovered, 'Thanks, Mayor Simpson! From now on, we'll all be taking golden showers.'

In England we had a children's animated series from the 1970s called Captain Pugwash. One of the characters was called Seaman Staines. Rii-ight!

More sexual idea seeding.

Come, come now...

Don't be too **hard** on her.'

We need to **penetrate** the matter deeply.

Create an opening for some new ideas.

That's a nice pair of X you have there.

Don't think **dirty** thoughts. (The word 'dirty' can be erotic.)

This **thing** is huge.... and ribbed – when referring to your barbecued ribs.

Having trouble getting **it** up?

Is that a gun in your pocket or are you just pleased to see me?

Are you an expert gymnast?

That's a big **sausage** you have there. Can you handle it all?

She **swallowed hard.**

Mine's bigger. I mean my cucumber is bigger.

You're taking **this** all the wrong way!

Talking about a female weightlifter, 'I saw her **snatch** this morning and it was amazing!'

If you were starving you'd eat **beaver** if you could get it.

The wife of the Cambridge President is kissing the **cox** of the Oxford crew.

Regarding a golfer, '...before each tee shot, his wife takes out his **balls** and kisses them.' Or, '...he felt much better today after a **69** yesterday.'

A British newsreader once said, 'They seem cold out there, they're rubbing each other and he's only **come** in his shorts.'

One of my favourites was from the BBC TV comedy 'Just Good Friends.' The ladies' man character asks his date,

'Fancy **a quick one**?'

She replies, 'I'll have a gin and tonic.'

He looks at her for a beat, a bit nonplussed,

'Alright we'll have a drink first.'

If you are a hypnotist and someone (not a client!) attractive says,

'**Do me** next!'

Or

'Can you teach me how to **do it**!'

You can say,

'Sure!'

Oh really; how smutty! That's enough of that!!! I heard you don't get enough! Ok time to stop. Get the idea though? Just a bit on fun with words.

WARNING: <u>NO use in therapy I hasten to add.</u>

But what do they do? They *bypass the critical mind* and *access the sense of humour and sexual part of the brain instantly.* Angry language accesses the fight or flight system. It's all state dependent learning and all an unconscious response. Remember: the unconscious runs through ALL possible meanings and permutations of words in an instant. These puns light up the sexual part of the neurology. *These are all examples of idea seeding.* You think advertisers etc. don't know this stuff???! Remember lustnosis? You get men through the eye, women through the ear or 'inner ear' with words.

Ok I was just doing some research to see if I was right about this: I am! I read some of '50 Shades of Grey.' Reading garbage is tough. I can see instantly why it was a success from the sexual imagery and use of sexually ambiguous words; that book literally puts women into an instantaneous sexual trance.

To wrap up: let's take at look at...

50 Shades of suggestive language.

Just looking at page 1-2 of this pointless book is enough. I'm going to list all the sexually suggestive/sexual priming words that seduced millions of women. That book actually f**ks women's minds. No joke. It is the most mind bending book since Lady Chatterly's Lover emerged pre WW2.

No grey zone: the sexual psycholinguistics of a bestseller.

In fact let's devote a short module to this. 50 Shades of Grey is pure sexual waking hypnosis for women; end and beginning of story. It's techniques in two pages alone are staggering, within a few chapters impressive in a cold, calculated way: they are?

- **Expectation/sexual anticipation:** The reader has been primed for a book that is about BDSM sex. It puts her in an 'arousal trance' in anticipation. Most people are a bit 'kinky' but full on BDSM is something different. Also the 'craze' phenomena creates the desire to read, appeals to women's sense of wanting to belong, more importantly to conform to perceived societal norms; being physically smaller than men women form 'friend groups' for protection. This has been extended by virtual online 'friend groups' like Facebook and Mumsnet. Christian Grey is like Moby Dick, no pun intended – the reader is awaiting this character's arrival! He is the post millennial anti-Darcy!

- **Sexual ambiguity to create arousal and foreshadowing:** using words and phrases like - <u>probing</u> questions, <u>cock</u>ing his <u>head</u>, shadowy forbidden places. The sexual and BDSM ambiguities used on the first 2 pages in a non-sexual context are:

Subjecting me.

Ordeal.

Submission.

Wayward hair. (Pubes? Wayward lifestyle??)

Succumb. (Think about it.)

These represent examples of sexual predictive programming. They are subliminally getting the woman aroused and in the mood etc.

- **Mystery:** Little is known about Grey, he has 'secrets.' How will events unfold etc.? He speaks in short purposeful sentences (this implies information withheld).

- **Fairy story imagery/age regression:** references to White Knight, Grey rescues heroine twice etc. Young girls are fascinated with innocent romantic fairy tales like Cinderella. This story warps that.

- **Blatant phallic symbolism:** Grey lives in a modern Dracula's castle; a huge skyscraper. It's a pseudo penis people: and it's *enormous!* Sex and power imagery.

- **Gradual acclimatisation to abnormal fetishes:** the author who is interestingly a very physically unattractive creature prepares the reader gradually to be sucked into the world of fetish; Christian's cold commanding aspect to his character (he is a bit MPD by the way), the fact he is a control freak, his purchasing of rope and tape at the hardware store the heroine works in (she is total loser by the way), the first glimpse of his BDSM fetish by the couple's first rough kiss in an elevator. This all prepares the woman reader's brain to accept the revelation of Grey's 'torture'/'love' dungeon which incidentally *numbs* the heroine – Plato described how Socrates would 'numb' young men through hypnotic questioning (confusion) to induce trance. The gradual preparation rather than the author just saying on page one – so and so has a BDSM chamber filled with pain inducing devices 'grooms' the heroine and woman reader for what will follow. If you want to break a taboo you must do it incrementally – to 'normalise' it. This is what paedophiles do by the way. The author says that the leather on the tables etc. in the f**k dungeon are ox-blood in colour – suggestive of a slaughterhouse. Sex and death connected – nice!

- **School girl imagery/age regression:** the heroine sticks out her tongue, has a satchel, twiddles her fingers when nervous, she does cartwheels in her head. This is young girl imagery – she is referred to as an innocent, like a child, she's also 21 but a virgin; a rare thing in these times. Seduction means 'to corrupt.'

- **The one forbidden thing:** *'Don't do it; he's dangerous!'* That's the best way to get a young woman to do anything! The stories I could tell you...

- **Description of psycho-physical-emotional response of 'heroine':** All absorbing books put people into waking trance. There are lots of descriptions of blushing, nerves – shaking knees, trembling hands, currents of electricity, shivers, tingling scalp, tingles, giddiness, stomach twists, butterflies in stomach, heart pounding, heart in mouth, dry mouth etc. This enables women to 'go inside' and feel them in the hypnotised state. These feelings are revivified/elicited by the text. In book 1, I outlined the hypnotic principle of fixating people's attention on bodily sensations. The heroine is turned into horny jellified putty at the mere sight of Grey; she has no control over her attraction circuitry. His mere presence makes those muscles down there clench! Now a woman reading this is going to experience it to whatever degree she permits herself too – all from vividly described sensations. 'Erotic' fiction/(post)modern 'romantic' (cut the crap it's woman porn) fiction is the number 1 bestselling genre of books on earth!

- **1st person/associated position of heroine (use of I):** The whole story is from the 'I' position; from the heroine's POV. This makes reader identification much more intense: she feels the emotions the heroine does, from the inside. In hypnosis you associate people into states you want them to feel.

- **Psychopathic traits of hero (the 'vulnerable psycho'):** emotionless, cold office, intently gazing, penetrating gaze, hooded eyes, control freak. He is frequently described as having a soft, hypnotic voice. The heroine says outright that she is hypnotised by him; and as with real psychopaths her friend sees the danger and she doesn't.

- **Use of Jungian 'shadow' archetype:** Grey is actually the monster archetype of myth but he is not an obstacle to 'love' (actually the heroine 'lusts' him) but rather an object of that love/lust; she wants to have sex with the 'dragon.' A warping of conventional storytelling/a taboo and thus mesmerising. The story represents a reversal of women's unconscious 'romance' archetype, which is to find genuine love and have children thus completing the human life cycle. Grey represents endless, loveless sex and no children: effectively genomic 'death.'

- **Hero as 'Lucifer':** Like Anakin Skywalker in the Star Wars films Grey is a classic 'troubled' anti-hero. He is said to be stunningly beautiful – as was Lucifer, 'the brightest' of all God's angels. He compares the heroine to Eve in the garden and Grey has red hair suggestive of fire. Grey represents a 'fallen angel' that the incongruously named Anastasia Steel (Anastasia – suggestive of Aristocratic blood/fairy tale princess. Steel - suggestive of strength) in turn falls for. Like Eve the heroine is 'rebelling' against what she is 'supposed' to do. This is a very enticing thing for the reader whose dormant 'rebel part' (see book 3, Powerful hypnosis) is stimulated. The heroine also signs a 'pact' with Grey; as in vampire films the heroine must agree/welcome/permit her own demise. Remember in Buffy the vampire slayer; you always have to invite the demon in before it can attack.

- **Use of repetitive and reoccurring language as emotional anchors (N.A.C):** Christian Grey's name is a repetitious cue for the reader to access the sexual tension state through the book. Also the heroine rapidly associates lifts/elevators with sexual arousal.

- **Mundane world replaced by fantasy world:** the heroine's life is dull, she is a young woman with very low self-esteem and worth; Grey offers an 'escape' onto a world of *real* *fantasy*. Fantasy is hypnotic; the possible fulfilment of a fantasy by a person like the heroine who is getting very few emotional needs met is like a hypno-disc: it draws her in – as she says, like a moth to a flame.

- **Linguistic foreplay or 'sexual fractionation':** As in hypnosis the author fractionates between Anastasia's mundane world and her sexual fantasy world. One scene builds sexual tension – this is abruptly stopped at a certain level of arousal (causing sexual frustration in the reader); then a banal scene follows, heroine goes back to normal hum-drum life. This is followed by more intense sexual escalation ad infinitum. The reader is taken in and out of sexual trance repeatedly so deepening the sexual trance each time it is revivified.

- **Conscious and subconscious conflict:** The conscious mind of the heroine sees all the trouble that Grey will be; but her subconscious FEELINGS (both emotions and physical

sensations) compel her to her doom. She is experiencing conscious/subconscious conflict.
Interestingly the author's depiction of the subconscious is very Freudian. It is not the benevolent subconscious of the Ericksonian model but rather a dark, destructive 'other' within, with its own self-harmful agenda.

50 Shades of Grey is not badly written, it is however cold, clinical, loveless, 'cynical' and deeply 'manipulative' of the 'female psyche.' The author is as insightful as a team of psychologists; each word, each paragraph and scene is deeply layered with many, many techniques that will inexorably draw the unsuspecting reader into a world that is best not experienced by the sane. The increased interest and sales of BDSM lifestyle and equipment following the incredible success of the book show the fact that ***IF YOU CAN GET SOMEONE TO VIVIDLY IMAGINE SOMETHING, THEY PERCIEVE IT AS THEIR OWN THOUGHT.*** There does seem to be some evidence that the book has proved the tipping point in already troubled

marriages. Oh beware of looking into the darkness: one day it might look back at <u>YOU!</u> Now let me add some scientific proof to back up what I say...

<u>Study proves stories physically rewire brain.</u>

The following is taken from a December 30th 2013 'issue of' News.co.au. The headline?

Scientists say great novels can change brain's biology.

No one with any taste in literature will accuse 50 Shades of dross of being a 'great' novel but...Everyone has experienced the way a captivating novel can make you **feel like you're seeing things through the eyes of its characters.** (Hypnotic association.)

This feeling however is far more real than you have imagined up until now. The latest study by scientists at Emory University shows how the **biology of a reader's brain actually changes to allow them to experience the physical sensations they're reading about.**

The boffins found reading novels can create -

measurable changes in the brain that linger for at least five days after reading.
One of the neuroscientists said they wanted to know how the story gets into our brains and what it actually does to it. The poor subjects were forced to read Pompeii by Robert Harris. On completing the drivel, toilet paper, I mean book, they underwent MRI scans over five days.

The findings?

- 'Heightened connectivity' in the left temporal cortex, the bit of our grey matter involved with language was still active 5 days after the book had been finished.

- 'Heightened connectivity' in the noggin's central sulcus, the main sensory motor component of that jelly blob in your skull. **The neurons of this region are involved with making representations of sensation for the body, something known as 'grounded cognition.' An example: just by thinking about or imagining running someone can**

<u>activate the neurons associated with running.</u> Do you see the f**%$*g implications!?

- The boffins concluded - the neural changes linked with bodily sensations and movement systems indicate that reading a novel can transport you into the body of the hero/heroine; *thereby indicating that 'identification' has a real psycho-physiological basis.*

Getting clients to imagine behaving differently, say confidently in a situation they were nervous in, is what I do for a living: it produces behavioural/emotional/cognitive change in <u>reality.</u>

Ponder this.

Advanced idea seeding.

The best way to idea seed is to talk about something similar to what you want a person to experience/act upon: what do I mean? Well you can describe how _someone else_ went into trance to get your victim to go into trance,

'I had a client the other day who wanted to

experience deep hypnosis...

They asked,

'What do I need to do to **go into a trance?'**

Not much I said,

'You could **focus on your breathing...**

it usually helps people **relax deeply, now.'**

I then said,

_'Don't try to listen consciously...

it's like when you go out and you're in a crowded place_

*and **you hear** someone say your name*

but they're not talking about you...

a part of you is always listening...

*it doesn't need to **SLEEP!***

Some hypnotist's direct a person attention...

to a pleasant feeling inside...etc.'

That will begin to induce trance obviously BUT you don't need embeds, trance language or rhythm to seed ideas etc. You can just talk about something related to the train of thought you'd like them to experience. So how can you do this in a non-script form?

Intention: You want someone to relax.

Simply describe VIVIDLY (use all senses) a time you relaxed or someone you know relaxed. Make sure you voice tone is calm.

Intention: To generate enthusiasm in others.

Simply describe a time you were enthusiastic about something; describe the enthusiasm of children (very infectious!). Do this with your whole attitude and tone conveying enthusiasm. I once did this at film school and 'enthused' everyone in my working group into making a documentary I wanted to make; this was when I had but a smattering of relevant knowledge on the subject matter. Unfortunately it worked and during the research period I discovered we should be attacking not supporting the people we were supposed to be making 'propaganda' for. Use your power wisely.

Intention: Warn people of a danger they don't recognise.

Simply describe how the majority of people in history didn't see an approaching danger but that an ignored minority did. Explain the consequences of that danger not being tackled early. Use a grave, 'concerned' tone. Don't use the fake concern of newsreaders.

I hope you get the idea by now. Talk indirectly about something that is like something else. Use as much implication as you can.

Nested images.

This is a deepener that uses dissociation and association to gradually intensify a feeling – this example is for hypnosis, you can use it for any feeling.

Nested images deepener.

(Hypnosis assumed)

'As you **relax deeper**...

just imagine over there

is an image of a you in a relaxing situation...

who is 10 times more relaxed than you are now...

When you are ready...

float into that more relaxed you...

and as you do...

you can **feel 10 times more relaxed** *just like that...*

(Allow 5-7 secs processing time.)

And again...

just imagine over there

is another image of a you in a relaxing situation

who is 10 times more relaxed than you are now...

And when you are ready...

float into that more relaxed you

and as you do

you can **feel 10 times more relaxed** *just like that...*

(Allow processing time.)

And one last time for luck...

just imagine over there...

is an image of a you in a relaxing situation...

who is 10 times more relaxed than you are now...

When it seems just right...

float into that more relaxed you

and as you do

you can **feel 10 times more relaxed**
just like that...

That's right!'

(Simple, quick, effective and follows
progressive 'rule of 3.')

Creating zombies: your waking hypnosis script.

This is a rather formal way to induce waking trance. I have shown you others in this book. If you have read all 3 of my other books you should be able to notice all the hypnotic processes I activate and utilise. If you haven't – go buy them! Ok...

Waking hypnosis script.

*'Can you just **focus you attention on x?** *(Candle flame, fireplace, dangling crystal etc.)

*And as you just gently but intently **look at it...***

draw all your attention to it for a while...

Nothing else to do...

No place else to go...

*as **another part of you listens** as you*

go into a waking trance

in your own time...

sooner or later we all naturally

develop an eyes open trance...

certain feelings can change within your body...

within your mind...

As another part listens

*you'll **feel calmer...***

Because I know

and each and both of you know

that we all...

go into a eyes open trance

sooner or later everyday...

like you did as a child...

Have you ever seen little children

when they zone out and go glassy-eyed?

As they take a little time out to

rest and daydream...

yet the eyes are open

because it's the inner mind that's

focused inwardly...

It's a bit like when you watch TV...

That's an **eyes open trance...**

now, *eventually, inevitably...*

when we look at anything at all

for long enough,

we **feel more quiet inside,**

we **feel greater peace...**

we allow all our muscles to **relax very deeply...**

because it is a quality,

a reality that as

you focus intently on just one thing...

relaxation of mind and body just happens...

and

we go into the 'zone'...

that's what some people call it when anyone can

ignore all irrelevant distractions...

and focus only on what captivates us...

you might say we

become profoundly absorbed

by what we are staring at...

as though nothing else is important...

when we do this,

when I do this I

feel inner peace,

there are no problems here

just perfect absorption...

in all ways we simply feel more comfortable...

and as **you sink deeper into that comfort…**

that state of pleasant absorption only grows…

it's funny because all these things just happen

as a result of just intently

looking at something…

so mental and physical relaxation are standard…

changes in the breathing rate too…

For there is a time to put aside unimportant concerns

for a while in daily living, is there not?

Such a healthy experience that you are experiencing,

experientially, now…

Thoughts just **drift away** *like little bubbles on the wind…*

going,

going,

gone...

in time...

on the inside

on the outside...

things quieten down...

the first sign is a relaxed body and face...

the eyes have perceptibly altered their focus...

this state of waking hypnosis only intensifies...

as a hypnotist guides someone with helpful suggestions...

and that's what it's all about...

you know a good way to avoid unnecessary tension?

It's to **focus on just one thing at a time...**

then...

everything can and
*does...**calm...right...down...inside...***

you don't even have to listen as you look

at that which captivates you...

hypnotically...

because some part is listening...

somehow...

just as a natural consequence of looking at
that thing...

this state intensifies...

more and more...

some people call this intensification

going deeper and deeper...

and that's fine...

just words

*that you don't have to **listen** too,*

*just too **still...***

and **quiet and peace increasing...**

as you drift off...

Maybe your imagination goes off...

on the most wondrous flights of fancy?

Maybe you remember **in a relaxing daze/days...**

times of total surrender to your own feelings of serenity, now?

Unnecessary movement is unnecessary in this place...

inside your daydreaming mind...

everything takes you deeper...

all experience serves only as a cue to

go into a deep state of waking hypnosis...

feeling so good about that...

and your eyes are open

yet you can **SLEEP DEEPLY!**

Such a blissful, serene state of mind...

of that body...

as you continue to look at x...

your hypnotic feelings only grow,

intensify...

now, when I...

count from 3 to 0...

with each number down

you go deeper into trance to a factor of 10...

10 times more intensely absorbed...

On 0 you will

be deeply absorbed in eyes open hypnosis...

feeling awesome...

Ready?

3

2

1

0...

Nothing...

peace of mind is yours...

you've zoned out completely, *have you not?*

And it feels wonderful

*to just **stay in this state for a while***...'

(You can do change work here with eyes open, doesn't make a difference for most people. You can set up a post hypnotic to re-activate this state on cue. *'Whenever I say the word **'sapphire'** you will instantly re-enter this state of waking hypnosis: this is a post hypnotic command!'* Waking hypnosis is no harder to obtain than eyes closed 'sleep hypnosis.' Play around with this stuff and improve on it with experience.)

How does this work?

1. Fixate attention on object.

2. Give suggestions for hypnosis as conscious mind is focused and therefore bypassed.

3. Main themes of suggestions are: **a.) maintain focus, b.) relaxation, c.) going deeper. These are recycled and reinforced in a circular feedback loop.**

4. Describe what you want them to experience and intensify/deepen.

This stuff is EASY folks. You can do it! *__What if you began to accept that potentially EVERYTHING can be turned into a hypnotic induction? How powerful a__*

hypnotist would you be then?! You know so many principles, far more than I knew when I started – now go play!

Note: if someone is highly hypnotically primed and motivated you can get someone to stare at <u>anything</u> and then start giving suggestions, especially in therapy: _so you can start therapy without the person knowing._

Rogue Hypnotist's NLP phobia cure.

The NLP 'fast phobia cure' is infamous. It is a very good way of getting rid of unpleasant emotions. Variations of it have been used to treat emotional eating, PTSD (Post Traumatic Stress Disorder) and OCD. If you are new to this stuff stick to phobias till you fully understand these others problems. It is also known as the visual kinesthetic dissociation pattern (VKD – sounds like a venereal disease). It is supposedly derived from watching Milton Erickson's work and/or it was *apparently* being used by those treating PTSD before NLP officially existed but who knows. I'll show you a more advanced method of getting rid of phobias in another book: it requires two chairs and a talented subject.

The following is said to dissociate the excessive fear of phobias etc. response so that the original 'phobic situation' and memory is no longer processed through the amygdala but becomes a normal memory through objective viewing by the neo-cortex. Could be, I have no clue! It works though. First time I used it is when I removed a friend of a friend's obsessive spider phobia; I remember him telling me that everywhere he went he obsessively checked for spiders! After this it was gone: I use symbology and authoritarian hypnosis to get rid of phobias now, but this should be in every hypnotist's arsenal. It is not always successful. I remember having an argument with a man who was religiously convinced that it always worked. I told him I had used it on one person and it hadn't. He looked stunned and said, 'No it does work.' He kept repeating this. Well, as long as he was convinced.

RH's 10 step NLP-esque phobia cure.

(Deep hypnosis assumed; before doing this - although not needed - you can set up a N.A.C trigger for relaxation and confidence by pinching a finger and thumb together: see book 3 for the mechanics of this.)

Step 1: create a safe place or sanctuary.

*'Now you find yourself in a happy, **tranquil** place,*

within your powerful mind,

perhaps it's somewhere you've been before?

I don't know – you do.

Or somewhere new?

It matters not.

Go there now **relaxing completely, feeling confident.**

(Give them processing time of 7-10 seconds or so.)

<u>*Step 2: set up a TV screen.*</u>

...I want you to see a small TV screen somewhere quite distant...

that **you feel comfortable** *with in your happy place.*

Notice you have a remote control...

and with it YOU control everything that appears on that TV...

On that screen over there see a black a white <u>still</u> image

(Note for hypnotist: it must be still, not a movie! Still images lack the emotional impact of 'internal movies.')

of yourself in a situation...

just before an experience from the past where you felt a phobic response towards that past x (x = whatever phobia is)...

(Note for hypnotist: it must be just before the triggering event not just after it starts because then they'll be accessing the fear!)

So it is a moment or two BEFORE that event began.

Step 3: double dissociate.

*Now **imagine** that you float up out of your body*

so that you can see yourself in front of you,

in your happy place looking at that TV screen.

It is as if you have become detached from yourself,

looking at an image of yourself,

looking at that TV screen.

That's right.

(Note for hypnotist: this double dissociation protects the client from accessing any phobic feelings.)

Step 4: watch a black and white movie of phobia run fast forward.

Now using your remote control,

I would like you to turn that still image

into a black and white movie over there...

(Note for hypnotist: black and white not colour and therefore not so linked to intense emotions.)

from this new even more detached position.

Run it all the way through very quickly in your mind,

*watching that situation in which you **had** a phobic response,*

a movie containing all the experiences,

*responses and feelings you have **had*** (use past predicates)

*about **that past problem.***

When it is finished...

and has <u>continued a few moments after</u> **<u>that</u>**
<u>experience is fully over,</u>

<u>(Note for hypnotist: it is of the upmost</u>
<u>importance that you take them past the</u>
<u>end of the phobic response to a time</u>
<u>when it had subsided.)</u>

freeze it at the end as a still image

or allow it to white out completely.

That's right.

<u>Step 5: Associate and rewind.</u>

Now that you are detached from your body,

watching yourself,

I want you to float into that TV screen

and into your body,

in that still image,

that you have just frozen or wiped out.

Now I'd like you to <u>run that film backwards</u>
but this time in colour.

Run that film very quickly now, faster and faster,

(NFH: say this next section very quickly!!!)

rewinding those seconds and minutes

so you are moving backwards very, very fast,

all the sounds backwards very fast with you in the movie.

All the way back now to the beginning BEFORE anything happened.

That's fantastic.

(NFH: go back to normal hypnotic tone.)

When you have done that

just drift back to your happy place from outside of that TV screen.

You are safe and secure *once again.*

Any time you wish you can make that ring of confidence* (*optional)

going back to that happy place and thoughts,

so you always remain in control.

It's not needed now so you can **relax** *your hand.*

You are totally safe.

Step 6: repeat step 5 with music.

Now, we can run that movie backwards again.

But this time you can hear some music...

that you find very funny indeed.

Anything you like.

The most ludicrous background music you can possibly imagine.

Ok now step or float into that old movie again (start to speed up voice)

and run that film backwards at super high speed...

as you did before but with that silly music.

Do that all the way back to the same place

before *that old phobic reaction occurred.*

*That's brilliant, and **just relax.*** (Normal hypno-voice tempo.)

When you have done that...

just drift back to you happy place from outside of that TV screen.

You are safe and secure *once again.*

You are totally safe.

(Pause a mo'.)

Now allow that TV screen to go blank,

just like that old memory which we have

changed in all the necessary ways.

Now, *get a real sense of how*

safe, secure and comfortable you are and continue to be.

Step 7: repeat step 6 two more times.

(NFH: Repeat running backwards 2 or 3 times if you wish: I would to be sure.)

Now, we can run that movie backwards again.

And you can hear your funny music again.

Anything you like.

The most gloriously ludicrous background music you can imagine.

Ok, now step or float into that old movie again

and run that film backwards at high speed (alter voice speed)

as you did before with that silly music.

Do that all the way back to the same place

<u>*before*</u> *that old phobic reaction occurred.*

That's brilliant, and **just relax.** (Voice etc.)

Now allow that TV screen to go blank,

just like that old memory

which we have **changed in all the necessary ways.**

No problem *(client's name).*

Get a real sense of how

safe, secure and comfortable you are and continue to be.

When you have done that...

just drift back to your happy place from outside of that TV screen.

You are safe and secure once again.

You always remain in control.

You are totally safe.

And one last time for luck!

Now, we'll run that old movie backwards again.

And once again you can hear that music that you find very funny indeed.

Anything you like.

The most ludicrous, silly background music you can imagine.

(Allow processing time etc.)

Ok now step or float into that old movie

again...

and run that film backwards at high speed (voice etc.)

as you did before with that silly music.

Do that all the way back to the same place

<u>before</u> that old phobic reaction occurred.

That's brilliant, and **just relax***.* (Voice etc.)

Now allow that TV screen to go blank,

just like that old memory which we have

changed in all the necessary ways.

Get a real sense of how **safe, secure and comfortable you are and continue to be.**

And...

when you have done that...

just drift back to your happy place from outside of that TV screen.

You are safe and secure once

again.

You always remain in control.

You can relax.

<u>*Step 8: associated fast forward.*</u>

Now I'd like you to run the movie forwards, (speed up voice!)

but with you in it again,

checking how you feel in that situation

*in which you **used** to experience that old phobic response...*

You can use your ring of confidence if you wish to   (option)

boost your confidence, unconsciously, now!

Then freeze that movie at the end...

and return to your safe place,

(Slow voice tempo – the tempo alterations spin the brain all over the place, 'frying' the brain, radically

changing the way it used to process information.)

looking at yourself,

looking at the TV.

That's it.

Per-fect!

And just totally relax...

Step 9: Future pace/rehearsal - dissociated...

Sitting in that safe place,

I'd like you to expand that screen...

so that it fills your entire peripheral vision.

It's totally panoramic!

Now, I'd like you to create a full colour,

richly detailed movie of yourself...

*being **fully confident and resourceful in that situation***

that used to bother you.

Watch yourself in it...

(Dissociated suggestion.)

You can include an inspiring soundtrack,

one that makes you **feel really good.**

That's it!

(Allow 10-15 seconds or so.)

When you are satisfied with it from this safe place...

You can you run it all the way through three times from beginning to the end...

everything going fine...

confident, indifferent perhaps...

...I'll pause a full minute while you do that...

(Allow full minute or...)

When you have done that...

nod your head,

wiggle your finger

or just acknowledge to yourself that, (covers

all options)

the changes have been made.

Step 10: final confidence re-enforcer - associated!

Great! You are doing brilliantly.

Now, I'd like you to step/float etc. into that movie...

and run it as if it were happening now.

You can use your ring of confidence if you wish to (option only)

boost your confidence significantly

as you experience confidence in that situation...

being so resourceful,

so totally confidently *from beginning to end.*

(Allow 10 seconds or so to process)

Now run that two more times making sure...

that you are fully 100% satisfied with everything you see and hear and feel, knowing that **from now on your are confident, strong, positive,** *handling everything amazingly well in that situation that used to bother you.*

Great!

(Be quiet for about 30 seconds.)

These changes are locked in solidly, permanently now, no problem whatsoever...

as you move forward

to your bright, positive, confident present and future,

leaving the past in the past, now...

That's right...'

(The still, black and white image, double dissociation, multiple rewinding, changes in voice tone and tempo, 'music,' fast-forwarding 'scramble' the way the brain processed the phobic

emotions. Afterward it does not, it cannot 'pattern match' to the old trigger the old way. THEN you build in confidence through future rehearsal: first dissociated then associated. Easy-peasy. Most courses charge you 100s or 1000s of £s or $s to learn this – you just did so for under a $/£ if you bought the kindle version. Well you're quite welcome.)

Bizarre MPD insight.

According to some therapists who specialise in such terrible cases, if a multiple personality victim is female and has a male alter it can indicate that it is/was a man that has abused/is abusing her; she 'introjects' the strength of the male abuser/torturer to create a strong, masculine part of her total self. Weird. Poor people.

Rogue hypnotist's unpleasant feelings dimmer switch.

This is a good trick for reducing other unpleasant emotions like guilt, anxiety etc. I would use it in conjunction with other stuff. Conversely you could adapt it to brighten pleasant feelings to make them stronger. It uses my principle of 'colour feelings'; see 'How to hypnotise anyone,' and 'Mastering hypnotic language.' Ok...

Unpleasant feeling dimmer switch script.

(Hypnosis assumed)

'Just imagine a colour of that old unpleasant feeling/level of x that you used to feel. What colour would that be?

(Allow processing time 7-10 seconds.)

Got that? Ok...

(This is rhetorical don't wait for a response.)

Now imagine you have a dimmer switch.

You know the kind you might find in a house...

maybe you have one?

I don't know – you know...

And using your powerful imagination...

somehow connect that dimmer switch to the old colour of x (unwanted feeling)

just before you **reduce that feeling...unconsciously...**

Not now but in a moment I am going to say the letters of the alphabet...

starting at A and working toward Z...

and as I do...

you can allow your far deeper mind to

dim, alter, change that colour of that old feeling...

so that it becomes far less noticeable, now.

(Don't mention feeling x directly from now on.)

Perhaps **that old feeling/response can disappear completely,** *we'll see...*

Just pretending this is so works just as well.

Ok you ready?

(You have primed the subconscious, it has a <u>plausible change ritual,</u> don't wait for a response go, go go!)

Here we go...

A – Starting to **allow that old feeling** *colour* **to fade now.**

B – Imagine that switch is being turned somehow and magically...

that old feeling is lessening more, now.

And as the old feeling goes, **this new calmness/etc. grows...**

C – Turning the dimmer down more...

And more so...

so that **the colour is even less bright**...*less noticeable...gradually...fading...away...*

D – becoming dimmer, less noticeable now.

Less of a bother...

feeling calmer...

E - And as you are continuing to more and more easily...

turn down that unnecessary feeling,

so that,

it's also easy to notice other pleasant,

maybe small or big changes that are occurring...

how much **calmer** *do you feel, now?*

F - This calming healing process continues in its own way,

your own way...

becoming dimmer, fading, melting...away...

much more pleasant feelings, changes occur...

I wonder what more positive things you will

notice next?

I wonder how **calm you become...?***

(*Yoda speech!)

G - I wonder how much more...

you can **relax into deep...hypnotic...trance***...*

Because the deeper you go the better you feel...

and the easier it is for these hypnotic words to steadily,

comfortably,

gently,

allow you to...

calm/etc....right...down...now...

turn down any residual feeling/x that you once had...

it's all changing...

H - How much more do you suppose your

powerful,

healing imagination can REALLY turn down that unnecessary state of mind?

Maybe just a little bit?

Perhaps a bit more?

But little things can make a big difference over time, can they not?

Or maybe just maybe, your imagination will help you to **turn down that fading colour** *more and more than just a little?*

I - Give that dimmer switch one final turn

as you somehow **turn down that colour** *a little bit more*

...and more...

or much more if you desire it...

J - **Letting that old feeling get as dim and small as is possible,**

as you **drift** *into...*

a very calm, steady, sure state of mind, now.

More and more and more so...that's it.

And this act can insure that,

these changes remain with you, now...

And that's that.

How good do you feel?'

(Sometimes anxiety etc. wants to go all in one go and sometimes it can take a few sessions; you can always repeat this, getting rid of it gradually, 'Fabian' style.)

Sales gimmick 1: *FAST* hypnosis.

Why is everything good if it's fast??? Quick as possible, fine! But fast? Hmmm? Instant inductions! Fast food! 5 minute phobia cure! Express train! Quick delivery! Instant downloads! We have all become so 'civilised,' so 'domesticated,' so completely impatient that we all want everything yesterday! SLOW DOWN! Fast doesn't always mean – comprehensive or long-term value for money. Can you hypnotise people very quickly? Course you can. But in some situations that's not possible. In therapy I have had very anxious clients who are terrified of being hypnotised quickly! Fact. Use speedy stuff only when it fits a client's experience, especially in their first session. Every hypnotist should 'invent' their own style. **The only reason to learn from anyone else is to 'steal' the bits that help and ditch the rest.** A lot of what hypnosis teachers say works so wonderfully doesn't in reality. The question hypnotists should ask is not,

'How quick am I?'

But,

'How comprehensively brief and effective am I?'

Sorry boys and girls but instant induction doesn't mean 100% therapeutic success. I am now at a stage where I always get 100% therapeutic success. Sometimes the subconscious wants to let go of problems gradually. Remember they've 'helped' a person get by for a long time. 'Coping mechanisms' are there for good reasons.

I've noticed people who favour quick work are also very succinct in their normal speaking patterns: they are brief and to the point in normal speech let alone in hypnosis work;

'That's correct,'

'Absolutely,'

'I hear you,'

are their usual short and staccato bursts of 'conversation.' More verbose folk tend to be attracted to Ericksonian stuff. If a client speaks rapidly, 'mimicking it' in hypnosis would match the way he/she speaks to themselves. Could be powerful. It might also suggest it would be easy to overload such a person's mind through talking a lot, what we call in England 'rabbiting on' (Cockney rhyming slang: verb 'to rabbit' – 'one speaking a great deal.' Usually used in reference to women. See Chaz and Dave music.)

Instant hand stick to test for high suggestibility and somnambulism.

Stage hypnotists need very good subjects – highly primed, motivated and highly suggestible people. Do the following to separate those who are in the right hypnotic mood to play with from those that aren't. This was the very first stage hypnosis trick I was ever taught. It's almost so simple it seems like it couldn't work but it does.

Hypnotic hand stick.

'Clap your hands together and squeeze them tighter and tighter!

(Simple command – don't ask – tell them confidently!)

*On the count of 3 you'll find it **impossible to unclasp them**!*

(In a moment pattern identified in book 2, 'Mastering hypnotic language.' You prime the unconscious expectation.)

*No matter how hard you TRY **those hands will stick together** until I say so!*

(Make it short and sweet. Use TRY – law of reverse effort)

1-2-3! **Those hands are stuck firm together!**

(The section of the crowd that does this successfully are your *willing* hypno-slaves for the night; their subconscious has agreed to play ball for your and their own purposes. Their entire body may shake as you do this skit! As I said this was one of the first tricks my stage hypnosis teacher taught me. It is so simple I doubted it could work, but it does! Embeds are not needed, he used none, ever.)

'Release!'

(Watch for those that do this too!)

Later on I break down how to make this hand stick stuff more powerful with anyone. The above is successful with some however. Note: as a hypnotist it is ENTIRELY unnecessary to do ANY tests to get hypnosis, but you can however learn hypnotic principles from such tests. These can be applied to communication in general.

Alice in wonderland 8 level symbology deepener.

Alice in Wonderland is a very 'trancey' book; lots of confusing hypnotic language and imagery. Let's take some themes from that and...I don't know if you've read Arthur C. Clarke's 2001, 2010, 2061 and 3001 Odyssey books? Weird! But be that as it may Clarke posits 8 states of consciousness. I have no idea if this is true but on the basis of the idea of it I created the...

Alice in Wonderland 8 level symbology deepener.

(Deep hypnosis assumed)

`Imagine that you are at the base of a great, old tree...*

it is very large...

no ordinary tree is this...

you see a hole in the bottom of the tree big enough to crawl through...

*and so you **go inside** that tree...*

It is so dark that you have to feel your way ahead...

All of a sudden you fall forward...

*yet strangely **you only feel relaxed about this...***

you tumble into a great hole underneath the tree...

*and you fall **all the way down...***

you free fall...

***in a calm state** of mind and body...*

as you fall, you pass ticking clocks...

grandfather clocks...

with their chimes

ding-dong...

small clocks...

and medium clocks...

even wrist watches...

and as you float downward passed those time

pieces

you fall deeper and deeper into this oblivion...

feeling only peace of mind...

some of the clocks hands are moving fast...

some are moving slow...

some are moving backwards in time...

almost as though...

time has no meaning inside this place...

All of a sudden the clocks disappear...

And a number 1 appears...

*you stop **drifting down, now** and you look at it...*

And beneath that number a symbol appears

that represents this level of hypnotic trance...

And...

I can let you know a secret...

as you **fall into this blissful hypnotic oblivion...**

you will see a further seven numbers going from 2-8...

and underneath them you will see 7 more unique symbols...

just floating there...

as you pass them...

each number with each differing symbol will represent

a deeper level of trance, now...

When I say...'Go!'

*You can begin to **go down***

seeing those numbers and symbols...

and each one takes you

deeper and deeper

so that by the time you reach...

the eighth symbol...

you will know...

really know...

that you have reached the deepest level

of a wonderful state of...

trance and hypnosis

that it is possible for you to experience, now...

Just seeing those curious symbols takes you

deeper and deeper now...

because they represent the keys to your mind...

the keys to your deeper states...

After I've said, 'Go!'

I'll **be quiet** *as you* **go all the way down...**

take all the time you need to **do this comfortably...**

and when you reach

the eighth level...

can you give me a signal...

such as wiggling a finger...

moving any muscle...

maybe twitching your nose...

just so I know

that you have gone that deep?

Or I'll just be quiet for a whole minute, which will be sufficient.

Ok ready?

Here...

we...

'GO!'

(Await the signal, if any. I have done this with several clients without adding the numbers but just asking for symbols, it works fine. Simplify, refine, improve is my motto with this work.)

My very own NLP pattern: the clown with a fish that helped a doctor!

I was once on an NLP in medicine course working with several doctors. Doctors are trained to be SO 'logical' that they generally make terrible hypnotists and NLPers. Why? They can't modulate their voice and put sufficient feeling in it! It's like working with Dr. Spock – cold and emotionless!!! This = failure!

Anyway I was working with an anesthesiologist, he taught me his NLP method for calming down patients before surgery. It only works when people see a mental image that creates anxiety as a result – like an internal 'horror' picture. This is what he did (it can be used for any mild and situational anxiety without hypnosis):

Remove anxiety inducing image NLP style.

'Imagine that scene that makes you anxious,

see it in your mind's eye.

Now imagine that image is a rubber image...

It's made of rubber, like an elastic band...

Now flick that rubber band away...

(Client does this. It happens quickly.)

Feel better, calmer?' (Don't ask '...is the anxiety better?' Don't mention 'it' after the change work.)

It was my turn to come up with something. Being a tad more creative I invented this on the spot.

Rogue Hypnotist 'Clown with fish' anxiety removal.

'See that image in your mind's eye that has bothered you...

up until now...

could be something from the past that makes you feel less than comfy..

it could be something you imagine might happen...

Got one?

(They respond)

Good!

Now imagine a ridiculous clown bursts onto the scene holding a large cod!

He runs up to everyone in that scene and slaps them around the face with that huge wet fish!

(Watch their reaction: the doctor burst out laughing! Instant reframe with humour! I didn't but you could add in...)

Whenever that image pops to mind you'll see that clown

slapping those people in the face with a cod,

so you can **feel differently about it, now.** ´

(Hypnotist 10 points, doctor 4. Use your creativity and humour folks!!!)

Waking hypnosis: coin staring, suggestibility tests etc.

All 'suggestibility tests' are forms of waking hypnosis that generally lead to eyes closed full hypnosis: here are a few examples. **Note - they are entirely unnecessary to achieving success in hypnotherapy,** as I said in my first book but I've plonked them here, a few at least, the ones with minimal or least props for your learning edification. Again – no embeds needed. The commands are presuppositions anyway, which is more than hypnotic enough for you.

Coin stare/smiley face button/badge stare.

'Ok have you seen people **go into trance just staring at something?**

It's just as example of how anyone can **fixate your attention and so enter hypnosis fast....**

Let's do something... (Who resists doing 'something'?)

Just look at that x... (Coin/badge/button/toe nail.)

After a while... (in a moment variant – also implies 'when you like')

imagine **that arm is becoming tired...**

like it has on other occasions, hasn't it?

And after a while...

that – x just slips/rolls/falls right out of your hand...

Just let it go wherever, not important now...

Like when you **fall asleep** *reading a book*

and you can **close your eyes** *and*

go all the way down into deep hypnosis, now...

<u>*Hand stare.*</u>

'Can you just look down at your x (knuckle/ring/nail, patch on knee etc.)

and **focus on that point** *for me...*

Like you do when you pleasurably watch TV...

(I give a <u>similar</u> example so that the

subconscious understands what is wanted)

and you

become absorbed as you look at it...

while you simply take

3 lovely relaxing breaths...

> (A. Overload. Two conscious tasks at once, both hypnotic. Too much to process.)

> (B. Just by giving a number you <u>presuppose</u> a limit to the task to be followed by another, this sets up expectation – these mini-trance inductions are deceptively simple.)

So on the third breath you

close your eyes

and **relax very deeply, now.**

Simple inductions like this can be used with children. See my caveats for hypnotising kids in book 3.

What colour is the sky today? Sending people on mini-trance loops.

The theory: *induce linguistic confusion briefly and then add a suggestion which is MORE likely to be followed as the person seeks to get out of confusion into something nicer.* You can tie up 'analytical types' brains with this sort of language to shut them up on the inside.

The practise: use only once or twice a session, it is not pleasant to be overly confused for prolonged periods unless you want to brainwash someone.

*'Can you consider what colour the sky is today as you **relax deeply inside?'***

You can use non-sequiturs (Latin – 'it does not follow')...

- *'I lived in a house without a basement...but I could still **relax about things.'***

- *'... just paying attention to your breathing <u>can make</u>* you **relax even more.***

- *'You can return to this room very soon, <u>bringing with you</u> everything you have learned in this session.'*

- *'As I count down the from 5 to 0 <u>you</u> <u>will</u>* **go deeper into healing trance***'.*

<u>*The above 3 underlines represent the point of false cause-effect. There is no LOGICAL connection between the just mentioned statements' premises and conclusions.</u>

<u>You can use surrealism...</u>

From (copyright free) **The Story of the Four Little Children Who Went Round the World (1871).**

'After a time they saw some land at a distance; and when they came to it, they found it was an island made of water quite surrounded by earth. Besides that, it was bordered by evanescent isthmuses with a great Gulf-stream running about all over it, so that it was perfectly beautiful, and contained only a single tree, 503 feet high.'

What about...

*'Stories are funny things you can **go inside as you remember a favourite one**...'*

Or...

'I can see nothing,' said Alice...

'My, you must have good eyes' replied the Cheshire Cat.

In Advertising the use of absurdity has been found to 'moderate negative attitudes' toward products and increase 'product recognition.' **_Surrealism sticks in the mind._** I came up with this gibberish...

*'How many purpley Martians does it take to make 10 of them? Considering that can take you **deeper.**'*

How can you use your own confusing language to distract the conscious mind for that 'hypnotic moment' and so **slip in** or **slide in** a suggestion? It's like prying open the drawbridge just for a second. Write some examples down to train the brain to do it naturally. Think nonsense!

Hypnotising bulls: bullfighting.

If matadors don't move apparently the bull won't run them down, they only charge the thing that moves the most, the red coloured cape is for the crowd, for the drama, but the movement does **fixate the attention**. It is the crowd that is hypnotised by the mad courage of the matador and the extreme and real danger that fixates humans. The horse mounted picadors purpose is said to be to lance the bulls shoulders so he is 'distracted and unengaged' ensuring he remains **focused on a single target** instead of charging at everything that moves. Clearly some kind of 'bullnosis' is occurring.

I can tell you how to 'hypnotise' a whole variety of animals in another book, to what end I have no idea! This reminds me of when young Milton Erickson was hiking; he approached a farm. The farmer's giant, vicious dog bounded over to bite the one day world famous father of sophisticated hypnosis. Erickson remaining calm used his walking stick and held it in front of himself with both arms. The dog, being a dog bit the stick. Erickson swiftly, powerfully kicked the dog in the nuts.

The farmer said something like,

'Never saw anyone best my dog before boy, come inside.'

If you carry out certain behaviours certain results will ensue. Being raised on a farm Erickson knew it would work because if you hold a stick out to an aggressive dog it has to bite it. This is how hypnosis works on humans: it's very simple – they have no choice.

What is willpower and how to have it.

In a nutshell: willpower is the ability to persist in pursuing desired goals in the face of obstacles. Most clients have little. Willpower is like a muscle and strengthens with use. Most people 'fail' for giving up too soon. Fear of failure is almost a form of irresponsibility. Many give themselves insufficient time to achieve goals. Given enough time you'd be VERY surprised what is possible. Now...

How to achieve goals without hypnosis.

The best formula is to work backwards from the future goal to where you are now and then work out what transitional process must take place for success to occur. This requires conscious thought and analysis.

Goal checklist.

1. Can I do it?

2. Is it realistic?

3. How long will it take to achieve it?

4. What will I have to learn to achieve it?

5. How much money will it cost me?

6. Will it adversely affect me or others? (Ethics, 'ecology' check.)

7. Is it a good long term decision?

8. What are the pros and cons?

9. Can I handle the cons? (Do you have sufficient mental toughness?)Etc.

Carry on in this vein until you have a solid idea of what is needed to achieve the goal.

Let's imagine your goal is 'become a Master Hypnotist.'

Step one: I am a master hypnotist. How did I get here?

Step two: I run a successful private practice.

Step three: I was a professional stage hypnotist.

Step four: I became fascinated by the subject of hypnosis and read all the books on it I could including old obscure ones. I learnt from lots of great teachers how to hypnotise anyone in varying ways.

Step five: I attended a clinical hypnotherapy course and got my professional qualifications.

Step 6: I read a few books on NLP, self-hypnosis.

Step 7: I am interested in learning more about hypnosis.

See how easy it is. Work back to front and decide what all the realistic, achievable steps will be. Build a solid wall, one brick onwards.

**Note: all budding hypnotists MUST be hypnotised to know what the state is actually like and how it varies. They can then talk to clients about it from personal experience: you can't be a 'hypno-virgin' and be a good hypnotist.**

To conclude: the main reason people fail to achieve goals, other things being equal (wealth/influence/who you know/power/opportunity etc.) is that they lack a real enough model of reality; operating from this unreal model they make bad decisions.

To achieve goals that are 'hard' you MUST be like the Terminator in the first movie. Obviously not the murdering bit!!! But no matter what is put in your way, no matter what others say (who cares what they think anyway? If they knew how to be successful they would have done it!), no matter how you get knocked back or down – you unrelentingly get back up again! You must be willing to be flexible in terms of strategy and tactics to achieve the goal if it is 'hard' and also you may achieve the goal and find out it wasn't as great as you imagined it would be. Goal and gaol are alarmingly similar! You then set new ones as you mature and develop from experience and hard knocks, which will occur.

The only exception to this is unrequited love. Just let that baby go. Get someone who appreciates you.

The Rogue Hypnotist's swish pattern.

I have found only one NLP swish pattern that works and it works better because I fiddled with it a bit. Swish patterns directionalise the mind – they are like a powerful visual suggestion. They say to the deeper mind: _not that, this!_

It can be used successfully with confidence, self-esteem/worth and minor habit problems like nail biting and smoking but only in conjunction with other things – it won't work alone, NLP things never bloody do! It's just another tool to 'bash' someone with to get them what they want. In book 3, 'Powerful hypnosis,' I talk about my 'overwhelming firepower' principle in therapy.

Rogue hypnotist's swish!

(Deep hypnosis is assumed – you can say this at a reasonably quick tempo – make it dynamic!)

Step 1: Setting up the alternatives phase.

'Think of what you are aware of in your past

just before you had a feeling, response or

behaviour

that you now wish to change about yourself:

see it as a small, black and white image

from your point of view

but some way off in the distance.

That's great.

(Pause for a few seconds)

Now, think of a 'free you' image – (make your tone increasingly enthused!)

a free you who no longer has that old response

you had **in the past.**

Now,

Look at it on a giant screen in your mind!

Make it big, bright, and very bold!

Make it wonderfully colourful and incredibly attractive!

Add in sounds and smells if you wish!

See yourself as you wish to be –

free, confident, at ease, happy, having fun!

Place that image behind you now.

<u>*Active phase...*</u>

(Pause and up your tempo...)

See that image of what you saw in the past

just before that old unhelpful response.

Black and white, small, some distance away.

Now,

simultaneously and VERY quickly

take the image of that old response

and put it behind you in the past

as you imagine and feel the picture of the free you

with all the qualities you desire

comes whizzing through your body

so that it now stands, before you

growing bigger, brighter, bolder

more colourful as it does!

Enjoy those good feelings and changes,

lock them in and

keep them permanently

as a gift to yourself,

now.

Relax, just think of a blank piece of paper...'

(Repeat the active phase two more times getting faster and more adamant, as though building to a crescendo. The last time you go through the process simplify it and say it with finality: as if that's that. Always let the client rest after each swish to allow them to calm down. Swishes are quite tiring for some people. The brain is being used and altered in a VERY different way than normal remember.)

How to remove an internal critic and what to put in its place.

Some people are tormented by an 'internal critic.' I brought this up in my third book, 'Powerful Hypnosis,' where I outlined some of my philosophy and approach to hypnosis and hypnotherapy especially called 'hypnotic deprogramming.'

What is the internal critic? Why is the little annoying b**s***d there at all???! Imagine you are told you are stupid as a child by an overly negative, critical, perfectionist or downright abusive mum, dad, a mean teacher, whoever. Now what if that person said that kind of stuff every day – almost brainwashing you through repetition so that that 'word-reality' was true – you came to believe it. So then your own brain starts to criticise you too, why not? You obviously deserve it! It may also be as a protective mechanism from abuse. If you internalise the criticism of the adult who verbally attacked you (and it is an attack, make no mistake) you can learn the rules of how to avoid criticism. Or so the child thinks. It doesn't work that way though. The abusive/negative person can never be pleased or placated because ***THEY*** are deficient, not the child. But that voice has been installed nonetheless.

What has happened is that we all have a 'part' that gives us feedback on what we are doing, tells us how to avoid mistakes but it also naturally encourages us! If you have been overly criticised (and all criticism is wrong because it is a global generalisation about you and not a behaviour) then you will overly criticise yourself. Nice. Thanks grown-ups! No one is globally 'clumsy,' but on occasion we can all DO clumsy things.

Now how shall we get rid of that yapping little s*%t in the skull???! It's enough that most people are quite negative, we don't want our own brains hijacking us too. One thing to bear in mind is to tell clients you are going to replace it with a positive, supportive voice. They can get worried at the thought of nothing being there, and rightly so, that voice has a positive function, it's just going about it in a really stupid and intensely unhelpful, self-sabotaging way.

Change negative voice for a positive voice script.

(Deep hypnosis assumed)

'Find exactly where that old internal critic voice is located...

most people say the back of the head...

(Pause...)

Ok, now imagine I have reached over and taken it out.

Now I am holding it in my hand   (pretend it's a squishy ball)

where we can more readily examine it...

I'm going to squish and compress this thing... (act this out.)

Make that old, negative whining voice as high,

shrill and unbelievable as possible...

Now you tell it in no uncertain terms to

SHUT THE F*** UP!!!

Or whatever else you want to say to it!

Shout at it in your mind, use your own words and swear words!

That's right.

Now you've done that...

you can **feel enormous relief!**

You just can't hear that yappy, sappy voice any longer.

Ahhh!

It does feel great doesn't it?

To **enjoy that moment of silence...**

utter peace...

blissful!

Now we are going to replace that

with this brand new empowering voice that I have here...

It only tells you positive, constructive, helpful things,

it supports you always, now...

It might speak in low, mellow, soothing tones

or confident enthusiastic ones...

whichever,

it always is encouraging you with just the appropriate level

of enthusiasm or whatever qualities

YOU would like it to have...

Ok, now, we are going to put this wonderful new voice

back in that old space.

Plonk! (Pretend you drop it in.)

It's a different voice coming from that same spot as the former one...

we have now removed, closed off

that old neural pathway

to those old limiting beliefs you once had,

have we not?

It's **gone for good now.** (Double meaning 'good.')

It's a much better new voice for you

in all the very many ways

you need and want it to be, now...

Examples of what it can say are...

'Well done!'

'We'll try a new way!'

'That was magnificent!'

You really are something!

'You can do it!'

'Yes, you can accomplish it!'

'This is how we'll do it!

'You can find the solution!'

'Go for it, now!'

And more and more than that, now...

And as that part creates that at just the right time,

in just the right way...

it'll be there for you as and when you need it, now...

And you can always hear it, when you do need to

in that soothing, comforting, confident, enthusiastic tone!

Continue hearing it this new way!

*Continue hearing it so **you feel very good!***

Do you want to go back to how it was?!!! (Tone should be incredulous.)

NO!

You can only move forward into your better future...

that you will create by taking action,

feeling better and better – even better in all ways

and in all situations, now...

And if that yappy voice were to

TRY IN VAIN

to intrude...

just let those voices argue amongst themselves

at an unconscious level...

BUT the positive one always wins!

It is always stronger, much more powerful, now!

It's solidly connected to the parts of you that move your life forward

to where you want and can be,

moving you toward the fulfilment of your unique needs,

towards healthy, natural pleasures,

happiness, natural joy and bursts of it!

To your confidence and success!

Laugh at the old ways of being now,

you're over that

forget it, move on now!

These changes can and will

remain with you...

working positively on your behalf,

guiding your permanent, purposeful

positive behaviours...

and always working for your highest interests

24 hours a day, 7 days a weeks,

It's nice to know that...

you have that security, *do you not?*

And you will, will you not? Will you not?'

(Note: this may not work on those who were severely abused; more deprograming needs to occur for them sometimes, but even with such people it can be a good way to at least start to destabilise the problem matrix - see book 3.)

Doing traditional hypnosis in the imagination: once more for luck.

Do this with a real hand mirror or not as I have below...

Imaginative hand mirror induction.

(Make sure eyes are closed, unless someone is good at visualising eyes open)

'Look at that hand mirror in your mind's eye...

as you look at your eyes...

straight into your own eyes...

you will start to notice

your eyelids feel heavier and heavier...

the more you stare into your own eyes...

the more tired those eyes become...

more and more tired

and maybe a bit watery as you look deep into your own eyes...

in your mind's eye...

that's it!

And soon **your eyes (in your imagination) get so heavy and tired...**

that they close and you drift off into **deep hypnotic SLEEP!**

Now...'

(Be quiet while they process this and look for the hypnotic response...continue with a deepener etc. Old time hypnotists favoured props like hypno-discs; let's assume your client knows what one is - so just get someone to close their eyes and imagine...)

Imaginary hypno-disc induction.

'As you see that hypno-disc

swirling around and around

drawing you deeper

and deeper...

in *your mind's eye...*

and when you **feel yourself being drawn** *into the hypno-disc...*

you will **enter a deep hypnotic state instantly...'**

(Imagining it may well be the much more powerful option; cheaper too.)

The Rogue Hypnotist's powerful self-esteem boost script!

Ok, now low self-worth, what it is etc. was covered quite extensively in book 3, 'Powerful hypnosis.' I am going to give you a very good method to boost it so people feel good about themselves: when they do, a great deal of change work becomes possible. They feel - they _can_ do it! It is possible because you changed their perceptions of themselves. It is derived from an old NLP pattern but with my own Rogue Hypnotist twists and added extras that you won't get anywhere else my padawans. Is this all I do? No, sometimes I have to do a lot more but this will work 99% of the time to your client's delight: and it is ALL about them at the end of the day. Here she is...

The Rogue Hynotist's powerful self-esteem boost!

(Deep hypnosis assumed)

Step 1: recall an unconditionally loving person.

'I want you to think about a very special

person in your life...

One who intensely cared or cares about you.

Who has had a wholly positive effect upon you.

Someone who would never misuse

their power of influence affecting you.

(NTH: Pause a moment to allow this; use your judgement.)

Perhaps allow a pleasant memory or memories

only come to mind of experiences with this special person...

I want you to intuitively become

deeply, profoundly aware...

as you **rest in this calm state...**

of all the elements that you feel contribute

to their being such a loving, kind person.

Develop a sense of what qualities, attributes

about this person make them such a loving, kind person...

Perhaps someone who has enriched your life

more than words can say.

<u>*Step 2: Dissociate person from old feelings of low self-worth.*</u>

Now, **imagine** *floating over to this special loving person,*

and take their perceptual position.

See yourself through their eyes.

Through the eyes of (unconditional) love.
(Any love will do but it's an option.)

Notice what qualities of yours

does this loving person appreciate about you?

What thoughts and **feelings** *do they have about you?* (Feelings lead to thoughts.)

Just get a sense of all that now,

this new perspective somehow empowers you,

unconsciously, now...

through the magic of hypnosis...

So notice how this can and will

appropriately yet profoundly

expand your sense of yourself

as a loving and lovable person.

Allow the knowledge,

the feelings of this experience

to **remain with you in a wholly positive way**

from now on,

influencing you positively*...*

and how you view yourself.

Tune into, see, get a real grasp

of your sense of this special person loving you.

Imagine *allowing this in a form of energy,*

perhaps a colour that

fills you with feelings of love and appreciation.

Notice what new,

better

more realistic,

uplifting

thoughts and feelings come to mind...

and how it also reflects

*these **new positive perceptions of yourself.***

Realise any ways that

this experience changes how you

perceive the world around you,

in this memory and in the future.

Now, *allow in a blissful way*

these wonderful feelings only to intensify,

perhaps the colour becomes brighter?

Or changes in some appropriate way?

(Allow some processing time.)

That's it...

Keep the feelings and thoughts locked within you,

only influencing you positively from now on.

Ok, that's great...

Now, you have locked in this loving and lovable state

that are linked to qualities that you

and others that you deeply care for

can truly, deeply appreciate about you.

Take a moment to **enjoy the contentment,**

the comfort, the kindness,

any new perspectives

that you have experienced about yourself.

Let those feelings of love, new appreciation grow,

increase and intensify in just the right way again,

doubling up that feeling of love and appreciation for yourself.

(Pause to let this happen.)

And double it up again – you deserve it...

you have always deserved to,

feel fundamentally good about yourself

and who you truly, deeply are, now...

(Again, allow processing time, say 5-7 perhaps 10 seconds or so.)

And when that's done...

you can

take this changing experience as a sign and a signal

that all the appropriate changes

in how you appreciate and truly love yourself

are now locked in forever.

Step 3: re-associate with good feelings.

Now, say thank you to that special person

and **easily keeping all these changes**

float, **drift** out of them...

and back into your own body now.

Good...

Step 4: Future rehearsal of success.

Now I'd like you to **imagine** a certain situation

on a movie screen over there,

in your bright future...

in which it would be so helpful to

be in touch with your own lovability.

This doesn't have to be a situation

in which you are guaranteed to be approved of.

It may be a situation that might involve people

who are not loving people,

or who don't appreciate you.

And now you deeply know

do you not, that

that's their loss,

you can't expect from people what they can't give...

Maybe you feel sorry for people

as incapable as that?

Maybe not, it's up to you...

but

you accept that...with some people that is/was so...

imagine being around people like that

but

see yourself behaving with an unshakable sense of your own lovability,

no matter what the opinions of others...

from now on

you validate yourself...

your own true self-worth as the unique individual that you are.

Notice,

how **you cannot be manipulated in any way or intimidated in any way,**

a person like that with that high love-ability level

that you are feeling and indeed amplifying,

at a deep, unconscious level

is secure in any situation, with any person

whatsoever

and this is so.

Because true love is not shaken by the changing wind,

it is as constant as the light of a star!

And you understand that

not everyone can recognise the worth of a precious gem.

and no one can be fully objective of themselves

or see what wonderful things others see in them...

and that's just the way it is...

and from this new perspective

and having made these lovely changes

can you...when you are ready...

when **you are happy and content, now**...

with that scene...

step into that you who can

maintain that deep self-love

and appreciation no matter what,

and **ramp up those feelings,**

that state of love,

of appreciation within you.

Double those feelings...

and double them again.

You are a loving person and this is so.

Deeply knowing this is so makes you

feel content, secure in this world.

So you know,

really know that you are and can be

that person that you truly are.

Step 6: the hidden gemstone symbology!

Now your far deeper mind knows...

that deep within you

is that

deep

profound

self-worth

that you were born with...

that is your birth right...

You are going to reconnect to that now...

Imagine that you are in a special healing place

called

'My inherent worth,'

in your wise and powerful mind...

I don't know where that is

but you do...

I don't know what it looks like...

but you really do, don't you?

As you walk through and explore that place...

you magically

strengthen and heal at a deep level...

and

your feeling of self-worth increases

more and more and more...

every part of your mind and body is

alive with this feeling, now!

And now

as you wander in this place

you notice a beautiful gemstone...

the 'Gemstone of your worth'...

you have found... (confusing Yoda speech)

notice its value

its true worth...

its imperfections only make it more beautiful...

see it glint and glisten over there...

notice all its qualities...

its shape,

size...

colour...

what type of gemstone is it?

*You can **feel a powerful sense***

of your inherent self-worth

as a good and deserving person,

a person who cares for others and is cared for,

who loves others and is loved in return

emanating powerfully from it!

Perhaps it inspires loving memories to come

to mind...

and the possibilities of your more loving future...

The gem contains all your uniqueness...

all your joys and passion for life!

So reach out and touch it and notice...

that as you do...

your feelings of self-worth increase all the more...

its loving, living, vital, real energy

enters you,

filling you with amazing feelings of worth

in a very profoundly blissful way...

Now, pick up your gem...

and place it to your heart...

and

let all those wonderful feelings

contained in that gem

melt into you...

flowing, healing,

going to that place inside

where it feels just right and

remaining there forever...

locked in even more deeply than ever before, is it not?

These feelings increase

more and more and more...

so that

you have reconnected to your birth right...

these amazing, awesome feelings radiate all through you...

getting better...

better...

even better...

people will notice the difference

and that's the way it will be, now.

So finally

all the feelings of that gem can

become a permanent part of you...

each and both of you, no-oooooooow!'

(That should do the trick padawans. *All good hypnotherapy/hypnosis and NLP dissociates clients from pain/discomfort and re-associates them into resourcefulness and pleasure.*)

We didn't start the fire! The weird history of hypnosis part deux!

Let's race through the hypnotic highlights of the past 300 odd years!

(1700s) 'Animal magnetism,' Mesmer resuscitates hypnosis!: Although the Alchemists, and weird odd bods like Paracelsus are said to have used 'hypnosis,' at least officially, it returns with gusto in Enlightenment France! Belief in God is dying and science is the new golden calf of the West...and onto this scene walks Mesmer, the 'father' of modern hypnosis. Now what did he do exactly? Well this mid-18th century Doctor from Vienna (Franz Anton Mesmer) was said to be interested in the '*esoteric aspects* of Western medical tradition'!!! This included the effect of astronomy, the planets and magnets on human welfare and behaviour.

Interestingly the 'conventional medical treatments' of his day were a mixture of bleeding, purgatives and opiates! **These were frequently more painful and terrifying than the conditions they claimed to treat.** *Sounds familiar.* The more things change the more they...

Mesmer claimed to have 'discovered' a will controlled fluid in humans which he could use to heal; like modern day suggestibility/hypnotisability scales he claimed the fluid levels varied in people. Well you did ask! Take a deep breath!!! **Methodologies: 'an air of mystery and studied effect' was created according to a contemporary's account. Our old friend expectation, mirrors (props), low light (narrow focus/sensory deprivation), 'profound' silence (sensory deprivation and focus on any stimulus), random bursts of music, (focus of attention/accessing unconscious response via music bypassing critical factor), a vat said to hold 'a heterogeneous mixture of chemical ingredients' (a prop and focus of attention/belief in 'science'- magic), clients/patients connected by cords, rods/holding hands (group hypnosis, making people more suggestible, focus on 'connector' – overload created with all the other competing stimulus),**

hypnotist then moved 'slowly and mysteriously' using a touch, hypnotic gaze, hand passes, rod pointing (slow movement = non-verbal fixation of attention on hypnotist and of 'slowing things down'; touch etc. = non-verbal triggers to enter trance, once 'response potential' observed), this was said to induce 'hysteria,' catalepsy, convulsions, rapid heartbeat, sweating etc. (spontaneous ideomotor responses, elicitation of fear/excitability trance, socially expected behaviour in context, witnessing others entering trance making it 'socially infectious'; very similar to overload principle used by cults.)

King Louis 16th commissions a 'scientific panel' to scrutinise 'Animal Magnetism,' revolutionary Benjamin Franklin is one of its number. Panel finds explanation of 'cures' in use of imagination and suggestibility: Mesmer is ruined. His 'disciples' keep faith alive. Needless to say I hope, we get the term 'Mesmerised' from him. Old Mesmer may have been a victim of the saying, 'That's all very well in practice, but does it work in theory?'

Aristocratic hypnosis - the Marquis de Puysegur: A French aristo de Puysegur used 'Animal Magnetism' to help improve people's moods. *The first recorded case of anyone attempting to do so apparently.* He used it to 'cure' toothaches. A young man called Victor, with what I can only figure out to be heart palpitations was brought before him. To the Marquis' surprise after a few minutes of chat the lad spontaneously went into trance! The boy spoke, gestured and was said to 'reveal his private affairs,' after which he was reported to have felt sad, the Marquis then did his best to give him a cheerful pep talk and hummed a merry tune quietly. The response? The boy started singing a happy tune out loud! After being left in this self-induced trance the boy awoke feeling better. I hope you can see the hypnotic patterns involved, they have all been covered in this book. **Methodology: expectation produces hypnosis without formal induction in a willing somnambulist. Talking freely = Freudian 'free association.' Ego boost therapy and**

mood improvement implied by humming a jolly tune. Very clever if you ask me.

The Marquis believed he recognised a relationship between some of Victor's reactions and sleepwalking, coining the term: 'Artificial Somnambulism.'

Late 18th, early 1900s: Abbe Faria's 'Lucid Sleep': Abbe (Jose-Custodio de) Faria was seemingly a strange character, priest, hypnotist and political revolutionary; also the inspiration for a character of the same name in Alexandre Dumas' 'The Count of Monte Cristo.' He tried to stage a revolution in the Portuguese trading zone (Goa) in India! He was thrown in prison for 20 years by Napoleon for his revolutionary leanings. **Oddly his book 'Lucid Sleep' has NEVER been fully translated into English.** He believed however that there was no 'fluid' as Mesmer suggested rather...

'Suggestion, which is an order from a concentrator **(hypnotist)***, is the immediate cause that triggers the real and precise cause that produces a particular and natural effect, but cannot produce it on its own. Induced*

lucid sleep, is a **concentration of the senses produced at will** *and limited only by internal freedom, but caused by the external influence of the* **concentrator's (hypnotist's) suggestion**...*Thus with* **mere words***, healthy subjects can be made ill, and ill subjects can be made healthy...All* **effects of suggestions occur in subjects not only during lucid sleep, but also in the wakeful state** *so long as they have experienced concentration at least once. Some, however, exhibit these aptitudes without ever having experienced, or even being able to experience, this type of sleep. Nonetheless, this occurrence outside of sleep is only partly like what occurred during sleep, whether it concerns intuition or the influence on body movements.'*

The highlighted sections in the above quote are mine. Do you see, everyone comes to the same conclusions? Pretty much. For a while hypnosis pops up now and again in odd little places – all seemingly French??? Was the 'hypnotic revival' linked to the revolutionary spirit abroad during this Age of Revolutions? Those like Faria who champion psychological explanations of hypnosis are known as 'animists.'

The first hypnotic Scotchman - Dr. James Esdaile: Esdaile deserves special mention in a period when mesmerists were busy debating magnetic fluids (fluidists) or those who leaned toward belief and suggestion (animists). A Scottish surgeon working in India in the middle of the 19th century he started to make hypnosis somewhat respectable; not performing stunts and variations of stage hypnosis as others had but developing serious hypnotherapy. So what did he reportedly do?

- 300 major and 1000 minor operations using only hypnotic anaesthesia.

- Arm, breast and, alarmingly, penis amputations (GOOD GRIEF!!!!), dental work and 'tumour' removal.

- Treatment of 18 nervous and medical complaints, including headaches, tics, convulsions, sciatica, inflammation of various body parts and a feeling of insects crawling over the body

Interestingly stage hypnotist's have induced the latter.

- He pens: **Mesmerism in India, and its Practical Application in Surgery and Medicine.** In which he summarises 73 painless surgical operations he carried out during his final eight months in the subcontinent.

- Unsurprisingly: never you mind the undoubted success of Esdaile's hypnotic anaesthesia - by the mid-19th century, 'mainstream medicine' favoured the use of nitrous oxide in surgery. ***There is precious little money to be made from using words to heal. Medicine is about PROFIT!***

Scotchman 2 (1840-50), Dr. James Braid makes hypnosis even more respectable – well for a bit: Although Scottish and possibly ginger (we mustn't hold this against him tempting though it be) Braid studied medicine at the University of Edinburgh, in turn becoming a general surgeon in Manchester, England.

Never before interested in hypnosis at the age of 46 he is a spectator of a 'travelling show' and witnesses a performance by a Swiss Mesmerist: he is mesmerised (intrigued) by mesmerism! He seeks to work out what it really is scientifically, through detailed observation. He seeks the permission of the Swiss hypnotist to observe his subjects and the hypnotist himself over a period of a few months. He cracks it!

He separates 'Hypnotism' from 'Animal Magnetism.' He said hypnosis was,

'...merely a simple, speedy, and certain mode of throwing the nervous system into a new condition, which may be rendered eminently available in the cure of certain disorders.'

What's in a name?

Braid labels mesmerism 'neurypnology' (nervous sleep) and pens a book on the subject. Next he tries – 'neuro-hypnotism.' Bit of a mouthful and doesn't really catch the public's imagination. Aha! To give the subject respectability Braid adopts an earlier French practitioner of Mesmerism, de Cuviller's terms:

'Hypnotism' and 'Hypnotist.' The first case of NLP like psycho-linguistics to reframe something feared and ridiculed?? He also wisely talked down its curative powers so as to gain further credence.

Let's look at one method he used: our old friend eye fixation. **Methodology: Get person to stare at a shiny object (small mirror, flame etc.) held a little above eye level; he described the response – contracting pupils followed by dilation. This is followed by what he termed a 'wavy motion' of the eyes. Then by moving the object toward the eyes of the hypnotee the eyelids flicker before spontaneously closing, i.e. fatigue.** For this he used no suggestion, just the non-verbal technique of eye fixation and physically suggested eye closure by moving the object of fixation closer to the victim's eyes.

He employed hypnosis in medical procedures including surgery to control pain, help stroke victims, certain skin problems, headaches and 'sensory impairment.' He later decides against the term hypnosis and prefers the term 'Monoideism.' Literally 'one idea,' referring to

the **fixation of attention/absorption**
required for inductions. People love showbiz
and mystery and it doesn't catch on. Hypnosis
sticks until the present day.

Late 19ᵗʰ century - the Nancy School:
Back to France again. Imagine a small general
practice in the French town of Nancy. Dr.
Ambroise Liebeault meets one of James
Braid's students and the infection is passed on
yet again.

Liebeault practices his new skills on his
patients ending pain and speeding healing. A
sufferer of chronic pain becomes his patient
and is cured. The patient tells his former
doctor of this seeming miracle, a certain
young Dr. Hippolyte Bernheim, a professor of
neurology at the University of Nancy. Dr.
Berheim contacts the older man and learns
the trade. The Nancy School is born: the
younger man authors the book 'Suggestive
Therapeutics' as a result. He identifies:
**hypnosis as a natural curative state,
varieties of trance depth** and **repetition**
as principles. Bernheim studies 'false
memories' and their implantation. He conducts
an experiment telling a patient that during the

previous night, his sleep had been disturbed by a noisy neighbour who spent much of the night singing with the windows open. When awakened and questioned about his 'sleep,' the patient recalls the implanted memory and believes it to be real - **believed in imaginings.**

Nancy's opposition - the Salpetriere School of Charcot: Dr. Jean-Martin Charcot violently opposes the findings of the Nancy school. A highly respected man he co-founds neurology itself! He runs the world's first clinic dedicated solely to the brain in Paris's Salpetriere Hospital (1882.) He is the first doctor to define: MS (Multiple Sclerosis) and AML (later 'Lou Gehrig's Disease'). He studies hysteria extensively and diseases which affect a patients perception of their body. **UNFORTUNATELY HE IS COMPLETELY WRONG ABOUT HYPNOSIS BUT BECEAUSE HE HAS A REPUTATION AS SOME SORT OF GENIUS MANY INFLUENTIAL PEOPLE LISTEN TO THE GIBBERISH HE SPOUTS ABOUT IT BEING A FORM OF 'HYSTERIA.' IDIOT.**
Remember kids; don't listen to 'experts.' Like

Freud who is to follow him he waylays the development of clinical hypnotherapy by about 50 years.

A 20 year research war ensues between the Nancy School and Salpetriere. In 1885 Freud witnesses the work of both schools and prepares to **ROYALLY F**K UP EVERYTHING ON A GLOBAL SCALE!!!!** The human mind is seen through a warped prism up to the present day. Hypnosis is not taught in most medical schools as a result of this mad man's 'theories.'

Late 19th early 20th century - Freud f**ks things up with Breuer!: Things seem to be heading in the right direction and then BOOM! Freud comes along and screws all the hard fought for progress up. So how does this start?

Czech born Freud travels to France and meets Josef Breuer, who becomes the former's 'mentor'; later the two become colleagues.

'Anna O.'

Breuer is treating a young lady who is said to have 'hysteria.' Her symptoms? Psychosomatic pain, 'speech disturbances,' lacking desire to eat or drink. *All signs of chronic stress.* Her symptoms worsen when her father dies. This is common as the death of a near relative entails a loss of our natural human needs for attention, emotional connection etc. (See book, '3 Powerful hypnosis.')

- Breuer uses hypnosis to 'relax' her.

- He lets her 'talk freely' in the trance state.

- He 'explores memories' that *seemingly* arose spontaneously within this state. (Did they?)

In other words he didn't know what the f**k he was doing! After two years (this proves it was unsuccessful, I could cure this in a single session) he invents his proto-ideas of psychoanalysis ('psycho-anal-cyst' as I prefer to call it); Freud allegedly develops these 'discoveries,' and invents his conversational hypnosis technique which he calls, 'free association.' I cover this subject in more depth in my third book.

Lastly we shall deal with Emile Coue.

20th century boy - the goatee wearing Chemist turned hypnotist:

Coue a chemist in France notes patients seem to heal more quickly when he **praised** a medication and left a **positive** note reminding the patient of the daily dosage (the placebo effect). Intrigued he hears of the Nancy School's ideas about 'suggestive therapeutics,' and studies with the founders (1901), soon after he offers hypnosis sessions to pharmaceutical clients.

After several years practice Coue comes to believe that 'conscious autosuggestion' by clients (self-hypnosis is born!) is best. He claimed he saw more long lasting results through this method. He coins the catch phrase used by the madman Dreyfuss (Herbert Lom) in the original Pink Panther films, 'Every day and in every way, I'm getting better and better!' **Repetition and rhyme.** He claimed...

*'Autosuggestion is an instrument that we possess at birth, and with which we play **unconsciously** all our life, as a baby plays with its rattle. It is however a dangerous instrument; it can **wound or even kill you** if you handle it imprudently and unconsciously.*

It can, on the contrary, save your life when you know how to employ it consciously.'

(From) **Self-Mastery through Conscious Autosuggestion.**

How many self-help/behavioural modification books did this man spawn without meaning too!? Here we see the power of 'hypnotic cursing' – the malediction, (literally bad-speech). And here my padawans ends our potted history of hypnosis: the history of 20th century hypnosis is to be covered in a later book/rant. In fact the next Rogue Hypnotist book called, 'Wizards of trance,' will uncloak the techniques of the great and some unknown 'hypnotists' of the ages.

The pleasure button.

Hypnotise someone using techniques I or others have taught you. Get them to imagine they have a pleasure button in their mind's eye; the button represents a release of pleasure. Get them to imagine pressing this button down and as they do so they will feel a massive surge of pleasure flooding through them. It's a nice thing to do for people.

Pleasure Button script.

(Hypnosis assumed)

'**Imagine** *a pleasure button in your mind's eye...*

When I say GO!

I want you to imagine pressing that pleasure button down...

and when you do...

you'll **feel an amazing wave of absolute...pure pleasure** *surge right through you...*

and it can **feel fantastic...**

Ok, here we go! Ready now! (The expectation has primed the subconscious to respond.)

'GO!'

That's right...

feel that amazing pleasure coursing through your mind...

and body...

and it can **feel wonderful,** *can it not?'*

I'm forever blowing bubbles: the 'Bubble Module' for inductions.

Ok now a nice little trick you can use to get the conscious mind to switch off for a bit during hypnosis is to create a visual construct or metaphor that represents 'thoughts' and then make them gradually disappear. You could use the analogy of autumn leaves on a tree being blown away by the wind or bubbles...

Bubble module for inductions.

(You can do this quite early on, say after eye closure, breathing focus and a bit of body relaxation and visualisation...see book 1 and 2 for full details)

'*Just imagine that some of those thoughts*

that are floating through your mind

are bubbles...

and as you **relax more**

and **become more deeply hypnotised...**

they can pop...

one by one...

or **float off into the distance** (a metaphor for dissociation)

and sooner or later

those bubbles disappear completely

and you **drift off into a trance, now...'**

The 100% success rate pain management script!

Using the 3 pain control modules below I have always had 100% success in treating pain caused by injury: surgical cock-ups, car accidents, the lot. Once you know this it will give you MASSIVE confidence in helping anyone who is in a similar boat, so to speak.

WARNING: Only use once the source of pain has been medically identified – pain is a necessary signal that something is wrong.

In hypnotic pain control we do not remove the pain, we **change the type of message sent and its intensity**. Reading the following will show you what I mean. You must install a post hypnotic command for self-hypnosis at home, so that the client/patient can manage the pain without your help. It takes 1 session 99% of the time. Unless the person gets overexcited at their new found freedom and reinjures themselves. Remember pain Is a feeling: you can use the principles in this to change any feeling state or create any pleasant one – if you have the brains.

Remember pain is often 'co-morbid' – it exists with another problem. Pain is made worse by fear, so take away any anxiety etc. Pain and depression are often linked, one leading to the other. Sometimes, very often, if you get rid of the pain the 'depression' lifts entirely. Relax people very deeply during hypnosis – this will help start putting good feelings in. Pain can make people suicidal; you may save lives with this information.

The Rogue Hypnotist's hypnotic pain control modules script.

(Deep hypnosis assumed)

Module 1: Healing colours (colour feelings).

'As you **rest very comfortably,**

here today,

feeling good,

so **deeply relaxed...**

comfort only *increasing,*

in a detached,

dissociated way I would like you to just

notice

those/that place/s of discomfort that you'd had

up until now,

but only in a way that allows you to –

feel little discomfort –

far **less discomfort, now,** *than you had.*

I wonder if you could put a shape or colour (symbology/colour feelings)

or both...

*to that old dis**comfort** before we –*

change it forever –

What colour/shape perhaps is it?

(Note: rarely some people discover their pain

etc. is represented symbolically by a noise or smell. If they do, go with it, accept what is offered by the subconscious without question.)

Whatever it is, in whatever way is right...

fully trust that subconscious representation...

What is it for you?

Notice any other sensations,

perhaps weight,

size,

odour or taste maybe?

Any sounds?

Bright or dim?

Near of far away?

*Many things can be noticed before we **alter it.***

*Really get to know that **now...***

(Allow reasonable time to do this.)

Now what would it be like if

you could imagine the colour

that would be there,

that was there before,

in memories of **comfort in those places,**

when there was **no discomfort,** *haven't you,*

anywhere but here,

anytime but now,

no discomfort,

only **comfort...now!**

Only wonderful comfort,

a comforting colour for you to

feel that *and only this.* (Confusion language used.)

Whatever it instinctively is, is right...

435

trust that inner representation...

is just the appropriate comfort colour for you.

It's your own healing colour.

It's perhaps new to know that you can put colours and shapes,

symbols...

even sounds,

smells and other things to feelings... (this is known as synaesthesia)

and when you do and when you have,

you can change it because you have already relaxed so deeply...

feeling calm...

What colour would we get by gently, artistically blending

that past discomfort colour fading...

with the replacement of your comfort colour

soothing, *spreading?*

As we get some of that past **discomfort** *to* **dissolve**

into that healing colour,

you'll notice it begins to **diminish,** *wasn't it?*

<u>*It's a kind of magic subsection.*</u>

(This subsection creates a 'construct': a healing potion that diminishes pain)

I don't suppose you've heard of hypnosis magic have you?

But it is real...

you will now learn how real it is...

So with that in mind...

Imagine *now a* **healing soothing lotion**

a **calming** *agent*

perhaps a bowl full of a certain something...

a soothing preparation...

poultice...

a **healing** fluid,

a **comforting** ointment,

a magically **healing** compound,

a secret formula.

Whatever it is for you

take that

healing,

soothing,

comforting quality,

knowing that there is a never-ending supply,

that comforts you,

now.

And in your imagination...

somehow...

and you know how...

that lotion/potion, whatever it is...

can find a way to be placed on that place...

that needs healing...

Maybe you imagine a nurse putting it there somehow?

Maybe a loved one?

Maybe you can do it?

In your mind, now...

the resulting sensation/s can be warm or cool...

and each and both are fine,

let it be what yours is...

*So, in your mind, imagine **you're hypnotically healing*** (ambiguity – your/you're)

solution is being spread

into the affected area...

I'll be quiet while you do

and

see it changing colour

from that healing colour to that mixed colour,

as the **former discomfort** *absorbs it...*

so that it is **changing** *in those areas*

that **had** *bothered you,*

to the new colour,

(changing pain signals *gradually* can 'pace' people's reality of having had a certain pain signal for a while and letting it go bit by bit. This can be especially useful if a client has had failed treatment after treatment from doctors who simply give drugs that make a person high so they don't notice the pain because they are too stoned!)

now

and you can **feel that calm, relaxed, soothing sensation, healing feeling...**

(Pause a mo to allow processing.)

Ok that is so good,

what a relief to –

regain control of bodily sensations – now in your mind...

And the result is magical...

almost as though you used a

crystal clear water,

just rinsing,

cleansing...

washing away...

that past discomfort

*that **used** to be in your body,*

*doesn't that **feel really good?***

And who weren't you really,

that feels comfort now,

anywhere but here,

anytime but now and in your future,

and only **this comfort spreading,**

as you **resolve a problem unconsciously, now...**

Now let's do all that again but better.

We need some more...

of that coloured healing substance

and again let someone...

whoever....

gently rub it into those areas that want it –

feel more comfort – now.

And...

notice what is happening this time?

The colour is changing less

or more slowly perhaps?

It's different,

because **nothing can stay exactly the same,**

always changing anyway,

may as well direct it purposefully for you,

that is because <u>there is far less dis-</u>

comfort only *there, now,*

to **change** *the healing colour, the next time,*

if it hasn't already completely changed,

beyond where it was, now,

the colour will hardly change or not at all?

Let's do that one more time for luck so that there is –

no discomfort left –

or so that **it is thoroughly diminished**

and altered *maybe to tingling,*

a new sensation...

mild pressures...

or warmths that indicate attention is needed,

so you are

free to focus on the many things

that captivate pleasantly in living,

so that **old things become of no great consequence.**

We need another healing application of that soothing substance;

now before we do that...

<u>*Noesitherapy subsection.*</u>

(Note: this is taken from Noesitherapy created by Dr. Escudero)

Imagine biting into a lemon

so that you get a bit of saliva on your tongue, just a bit.

Now, somehow spread your healing unction...

and allow it into those places that deeply need it...

and soothingly,

soothingly...

soothingly...

spread it into those places and

notice the healing colour now dominates so completely...

that the old colour vanishes

with beneficial consequences,

so much pleasure available, inside,

focus on the pleasure more and more, now and in your future.

Beautiful, you did that wonderfully.

Setting up 'home' management subsection.

You are learning the power of your subconscious

as you communicate with it new, improved ways, now...

You will be able to do whatever you need just by relaxing yourself,

just as you have and just do what we have done here,

using the self-hypnosis,

(I give pain control clients a post hypnotic command that only I and they know to go into deep hypnosis on cue to enable self-management at home etc.)

relaxation techniques that you've already experienced,

and each time you do the benefits last even longer,

that healing unction/cream etc. is always there for you,

whenever you need it.

Or if you wish you can

imagine a lemon get a bit of saliva and say —

'I feel abundant comfort,' –

and

you will experience that pleasant feeling of comfort where and when you need it.

(I set this up so someone has a mechanism to deal with unexpected pain. When you have saliva on your tongue the brain thinks you are safe and calm. Dry mouth is associated with stress and pain. You fool the brain's detection systems.)

Control room subsection.

(You can create 'control room' constructs to help with many problems: I have even used them to aid in lessening a nervous twitch)

You can imagine a control room in your mind...

In that room is a control panel that controls all sensations...

and when you wish to you can adjust any dials,

knobs...

buttons...

levers etc.

in such a way that...

it will **allow these comfortable**

feelings to increase.

These are post...hypnotic...commands.'

Module 2: Ignoring pain and reconfiguring it.

(This module re-directionalises the mind to feeling well/normal habitually not just for a short time. I have no idea how pain is 'created' by the nervous system/brain etc.; I have no need to. The following serves as a plausible ritual from which the subconscious makes the required adjustments. 'Portals' etc. are merely metaphors for 'unconscious alterations')

'We know that that construct that is called 'pain' (pain *is* a malleable construct)

is really felt in certain areas of the brain,

(a list of past predicates follow with the implication that the client is over this problem; these are not strictly embeds but you can emphasise them if you wish. The subconscious will act on them without emphasis as temporal presuppositions)

and you can know that that part had been

doing *its job perfectly.*

*Sending you appropriate warning signals in the **past**.*

*The place which seems to have **felt** that past discomfort...*

*is just the place where there **was** a problem,*

and the body's response to the problem is to alert your brain

*to something that **could** be wrong,*

*so it needed attention **then**.*

*You already **knew** that something was wrong,*

and you also know that

it had been given all the attention it can from you

and others.

In many ways that delivery system

is very simple and effective but may not realise that

– you no longer need to feel that

past discomfort that you had had.
(Double 'had' is deliberate, mildly confusing.)

*There is therefore no purpose to being
reminded it was there,*

so it is all right,

it's healthy and fine

that we can

find some new ways,

that you always had,

to lower,

weaken,

to appropriately alter perhaps

maybe even to the point where

you can feel amazing comfort.

Perhaps just to the stage that it is just

a tingling,

a warmth,

a light pressure maybe

or another **more comfortable signal**

that the subconscious can send when genuinely needed

and only then.

A message (sounds a bit like massage) *that protective action is required,*

that new response is what you can and will feel,

if you think about it,

or maybe so that you have to think about it in order to recall

that **it was there** *in the first place.*

You can quite **happily forget to remember**

that you ever had that discomfort,

in quite the way you **had** *experienced,*

and you and you could

begin to wonder

if it ever was there in that way that it **was**

in the first place

knowing that **discomfort is just a construct,**

an old communication that can **change,**

or whether it would be better to simply **forget that you ever had it.**

Now, *if you are silly and careless that old signal will come back...*

so take it easy...

(trust me: add in this warning. Some clients have been effectively crippled/disabled by pain and have been forced to lead highly restricted lives. Once free some go crazy and act as if they aren't injured and end up at square 1 again)

don't overdo it...

Or maybe we can simply

make it difficult for those former warnings to even reach the parts they did...

in the first place.

To do that, it is only necessary to recognise that there are many,

many portals/avenues for those particular **past discomfort flags**

to pass through,

along this way...

and that way...

up there...along...

before they even reach their destination...

and your subconscious mind can begin to

close those portals to that

or those particular areas,

wherever that was.

And where and when aren't you, that can

(complex negation)

only feel comfort spreading wonderfully,

throughout their life and body,

more and more and more,

everywhere you need it,

everywhere but back then,

anytime appropriate and

only that comfort growing too.

Even as I speak to you in **deep hypnotic sleep**

this is happening, beginning to

close the portals

that were for any appropriate area of past discomfort.

Each entry point **stopping more of the old signal,**

each gate that closes

allowing an increasing

feeling of comfort within your body

as new choices or new messages or improved ones that feel better,

sending better messages,

so many ways available,

and I don't know if you will

experience incredible comfort *as a cool comfort,*

or as a gently warming and healing sensation,

maybe a tingle or something of subconscious,

unconsciously choosing now,

either or anyway today

and in your future it is

a soothing, relaxed and comforting feeling.

Your subconscious knows what is right for you

and as it **closes certain portals**

in the pathways of old signals

so that

you can become steadily more aware

of the steadily **increasing levels of comfort,**

that feeling,

that **comfort feels so good to you,**

keep it as a gift to yourself.

Bring back **comfort and comfortable sensations to certain parts** *too.*

As that **old discomfort disappears** *and* **finally,** *at last,*

the comfort manages to reach that

particular area of your inner self to

turn off the old signal for the new, now...

Your subconscious is fully in charge,

it can choose,

decide

whether to experience the old sensations...

*or whether to recognise that **it has served its purpose,***

done its job,

*and just **let it go** as that **sense of comfort within your body steadily increases,***

so that and only that occurs,

and you begin to

remember more and more vividly

with lifelike familiarity...

the way you used to be able to feel

before that past discomfort,

you remember *so vividly and pleasurably, now...*

in fact you can recall it with crystal clarity that you could,

will, can you not? (Confusion!)

*That **that old message has faded away, right away,***

*into the background as you **focus upon the right way...***

*You know how and who to **feel very good...'***

Step 3: Pain tolerance module.

'There is a tremendous amount of...

learning you have acquired...

during your lifetime of experience in...

developing anaesthesias

throughout your entire body,

*like when mummy kissed it **better and is was.***

Discomfort has a positive function

it serves as feedback,

but you had forgotten the shoes on your feet

and then you were aware,

your top on your arm ('bad' English is deliberate and confusing)

and then you were aware.

An entertaining episode,

a learning can make us **forget things**

but a boring lesson at school made the chair feel hard,

natural anaesthesias occur

you sense things

and then you don't

as **awareness is pleasurably absorbed.**

No drugs...

external aids un-required... (I know 'un-required' is not a word *officially* : it's hypno-nonsense)

just the lifelong learnings you have

that have allowed you to

automatically turn sensations, warmths and pressures off

and on again...

imagine a colour of discomfort

changes to **a colour of comfort** *and* **soothes** *that which needs it,*

that's right,

unconsciously, now.

My nephew fell and hurt himself...

he was upset till he started watching Scooby Doo.

My nephew loves Scooby Doo...

and he just forgot about things and felt better, now...

The great hypnotist Milton Erikson asked a

woman

*if she would be concerned about her **feeling** of past dis-**comfort***

if she saw a tiger...

and she said

'No.'

And somehow the past discomfort was controlled,

unconsciously,

with a vast treasure trove of unconscious learnings now.

Like when we were little and we fell and mummy/daddy

*kissed it **all better and it was...***

and we just started to play,

almost like magic, wasn't it?

Hypnosis magic, nooooo-ooooow!'

Why the 'work ethic' k-ills people and the neglected importance of the natural human life cycle: why living it makes you healthy.

The people who are more likely to get mental health problems are perfectionists who work too hard and those who fail to follow the natural human life cycle. Erickson would know his patients had healed when they got a boyfriend/girlfriend/got married, got a job (not even one they liked) and had children; that was his criteria for success and there is lot of validity to that in this cultural system.

People are often stressed and become my clients when they feel blocked, 'stuck' and prevented from moving through this natural life process of maturation/independence/mate selection/child rearing. Social changes in the last 50 years act against these natural human desires and cause bad mental health. I don't care what anyone else says or believes I have seen the evidence first hand. I learn from my own experience and observations of reality.

But there's more: the work ethic if taken to extremes will kill you! Overwork, less time spent with family due to odd shifts, longer hours, poor work conditions and remuneration, a sense of 'making a difference' are all causes of worsening mental health; these (whatever you political views/delusions) are as a result of the total corporate takeover of the world (private monopoly), the destruction of independent small businesses ('mom and pop' stores in the US) and the de-unionisation of labour; unionised workers have better terms and conditions: fact.

The instability caused by the above leads to poor mental health, whether you like it or not. One of the good things about the Protestant work ethic was the idea of being independent through savings. The fact that post war Baby Boomers lost their Depression fear suckered them and their children into taking on massive debt. I have yet to meet a client of ordinary means who has not said in recent years that they and their families are struggling financially. What a world!

I will leave you with this thought: work hard or work smart? Discuss.

Why herbal remedies can be dangerous.

Amongst 'alternative' health care fans there is a great faith in 'herbal' remedies. This is essentially the use of plant vs 'chemical,' 'manmade' medicines. But plants are not all touchy feely things: some of these 'natural remedies' can be incredibly dangerous with just as bad 'side-effects' (just effects). Plants have been used as poisons for as long as man has been around. **The fear of pharmacology can lead to an either or mentality – the fact is you have to be very careful what you put inside your body, no matter what siren tune the sales hype sing.** Remember people peddling herbal cures are business people too. It doesn't mean plant based remedies can't be useful, it does mean you have to be very careful. *Do thorough research.*

Electrocuting us sane: totally mad ideas about electricity and good mental health???

If you were feeling a bit down in the dumps would you stick your wet finger in a plug socket? I hope the answer is no for your sake. Yet for a long time in the first and middle part of the twentieth century many shrinks convinced 'mentally ill' patients that being electrocuted would make you 'A OK' Sonny Jim! What won't people believe? As a therapist the first victim of electrocution 'therapy' I encountered was a poor man who had had lifelong debilitating depression caused by an evil mother who had made his life hell and programmed his mind in the most horrible of ways. As a result of being legally struck by lightning he lost all his short term memory (cannabis has a similar effect). He didn't report feeling much better after being zapped. Well there's a shocker! No pun intended. And the scary thing is being electrocuted, which is used in many brainwashing methodologies is making a comeback!

This form of legalised physical assault, for that

is what it is, actually induces a grand mal epileptic fit. It is interesting that this treatment found favour in Mussolini's Italy around the late 1930s. Hmmmm? A certain Dr. Cerletti was passing an abattoir and noticed pigs were electrocuted till unconscious before slaughter. He reasoned in an 'epiphany' that you could do the same to people to cure them of severe mental illness. He also injected patients with a 'suspension' of electroshocked pig brain!!! Results in good old Fascist Italy were said to be encouraging. *Note: who might be depressed and regarded as mentally ill in a dictatorship?* Political dissidents etc.? Just a thought.

Want to know something more as we continue in this macabre vein? Electrocution wasn't really used extensively until word got out that zapping the brains of 'dissidents' (sane people) in the Soviet Union had the effect of making them more pliable and 'happier' citizens; in a burst of curative enthusiasm the shrinks of the West decided maybe they should zap the mentally ill. **Who is more insane, a man who says he'll make you better by sending 10,000 volts through**

you or a person who is depressed?

Letters on a postcard. I did warn you about 'experts' in book 3.

Do you know that even up until the 1970s in the US you could be zapped for daydreaming too much!? Chilling. Remember the film 'One flew over the Cuckoo's Nest?' If not go watch it; even if the writer was mad it is an excellent story. The word 'Taser' represents a great reframe – 'human cattle prod' would be more appropriate like in George Lucas's sci-fi Dystopia THX1138. *Life imitates B movies!*

A Mad Hatter's world: 'Oh we're all quite mad around here.'

'I think it's kinda funny, I think it's kinda sad, the dream in which I'm dying is the best I ever had; mad world...' so rings the song's refrain and is it far from the truth? I remember listening to John Cleese of Monty Python, Basil Fawlty fame say he originally thought that most people were sane and just a few crazies were lurking about; but he said as he aged and grew wiser he realised that most people were mad and only a few sane.

'But I don't want to go among mad people,' Alice remarked.

'Oh, you can't help that,' said the Cat: 'We're all mad here. I'm mad. You're mad.'

'How do you know I'm mad?' said Alice.

'You must be,' said the Cat, 'Or you wouldn't have come here.'

Just something to ponder. Of course it depends on what you mean by 'mad.'

Skinner's baby box.

In the last book I attacked Freud with facts, now let's swiftly debunk B.F. Skinner one of the founders of 'behaviourism.'

I'd like to draw your attention to another example of why you should be SO careful who you learn (cough) 'therapeutic' techniques from. It is little known that this top 'behaviourist' kept his little baby girl in an almost sound proof box, it looked like a big hamster's cage with a plastic see-through panel. There are many images online of this lovely little girl locked in a box on her own for hours a day. Hmmm? What kind of 'person' does that to their own child???! It's a rhetorical question.

How to do self-hypnosis so it actually works!

Quick one this – self-hypnosis is NOT hypnosis, its auto-suggestion. This is the conscious mind giving the subconscious ideas in a relaxed and focused state. *Problem is this means the conscious mind is still online!* The total antithesis of true hypnosis. Auto-suggestion works over time but why bother through repetitive indoctrination? You want reasonably quick and effective results don't you?

Hetero hypnosis (being hypnotised by another) is always best; so how do you do 'self-hypnosis' then? Record your own hypnotic induction with the required suggestions! Easy. You could probably do it on most home computers etc. these days. ***As long as it trusts you*** the subconscious will likely act on your own voice readily; after all it hears it yapping away all day long. It's the voice in your head! If your subconscious and conscious mind are out of rapport the subconscious may well reason, 'I've been trying to guide that twerp for years and now it wants me to follow it's orders??! No thanks!'

If you are like the man I saw who thought his conscious brain ran everything through 'logic' (oh dear!) then your subconscious probably won't act on your suggestions because it'll think you are an intense idiot. If you 'believe' your conscious mind has to run everything you will totally exhaust yourself! This belief/delusion/idiocy had given him a generalised anxiety disorder, a nervous breakdown and chronic fatigue! He had tried to stop his breakdown by staring at things: waking hypnosis. This is like putting a plaster on a leg that is hanging off after a lion attack.

The conscious and unconscious metaphor.

'There is a castle surrounded by a moat. The castle guards can't just let in any old riff-raff. The guards only see the 'world' through tiny arrow slits. They only lower the draw bridge to allow communication with the king if there is no danger to the king or castle. If the guards suspect danger the drawbridge remains up.'

State dependent learning to induce trance.

'Hypnosis' is our natural learning state. It is the state in which we 'become absorbed' and so easily absorb information. Here is a very short script to access this learning state for hypnosis. If we learn in a relaxed state we are better at performing and retrieving the information that we learnt in that state. To prove this, get mildly drunk and watch something educational. Try to remember the info next morning. You might not remember anything but the gist of things. I accept no liability if you do this when revising for exams etc.

State dependent learning conversational hypnosis script.

'Have you ever learnt something incredibly interesting?

So much so that you **become fascinated...**

by this learning process;

so you just absorbed everything so easily...

It was probably a time when you

focused in...

Maybe on what someone was saying...

Maybe on what you were reading...

Perhaps while learning...

the component parts of a physical skill

because for that

you need to **concentrate...**

the reason is

most people need to **be relaxed to learn...**

what they need to **learn...**

here and now...

and when they **go into that learning state...**

they can **recall the relevant information easily, now...'**

Why 'meditation' can be dangerous.

Meditation can be dangerous: for some people it does indeed help them relax, for others it just makes them lethargic and groggy, in others still it can produce delusions. Some people who meditate excessively end up believing they are being obsessed by demons and experience psychotic breaks! Certain breathing patterns taught in meditation classes are sufficient to produce these delusional states. People can at the least start feeling spacey and weird and dissociated with regular meditation, especially the TM (Transcendental Meditation) variety.
Meditation is a bit like drugs; some people can handle it, some can't. You've been warned.
TM is a cult.

The man who thought he was only a conscious mind.

When does hypnosis start? At the point of first contact with a client. For ease of teaching we say hypnosis proper begins when you say 'close your eyes' but it begins with your first communication with a client/hypnotee. I had a client who believed his conscious mind was running the show as I have said already: he was a total a***h**e! He had seen shrinks, psychologists (one of who electrocuted his fingers to make him better!!!); everything they did failed. He was despairing of cure. These repeated 'failures' had convinced him nothing would work. He insisted that he meet me first to ascertain whether what I would do would work; even though his assumptions and conscious judgement of what would work had proved disastrously wrong thus far. He also had no knowledge of hypnosis, so his premise was illogical.

In the first email he sent he carefully catalogued his and others failures and he asked if I could *really* help. I replied, yes in one session and if it didn't work he didn't have to pay. He wrote back saying he admired my confidence! But it wasn't confidence, it was certainty. I had successfully helped numerous people with the same problems and I am a very experienced therapist. As a nonprofessional he was in no way capable of assessing if what I did would work: he had no training or knowledge and drew conclusions from a whole host of faulty assumptions. But I set up the whole hypnotic expectation of the elimination of his symptoms and thankfully we were successful.

The point is? Tell your clients who will have had failure after failure that YES you can help them and it will be easy. *Just make sure that you know how!* Get them excited about being free of those horrible, tormenting problems and you will marshal all their unconscious healing forces to their aid. This is the linguistic elicitation of the 'placebo' affect.

People undergoing surgery will often be depressed afterward: this is because although the conscious is anaesthetised the subconscious is wide awake with no firewall, so whatever stupid, clumsily worded c**p that comes out of the surgical team's mouth is taken literally. Doctors need to mind their language with as much care to 'linguistic hygiene' as they do to sterilising equipment. **Is it better to 'give' people false hope than 'certain' despair? Undoubtedly yes.**

How to communicate with a stubborn part.

The word stubborn is of unknown origin apparently, it is possibly derived from Old English 'stybb' – 'stump of a tree.' Something immovable.

The 'stubborn part' (only a metaphor folks for various unconscious processes) controls what you will do and what you won't do. You might say it has a list of what is permissible and a list of taboos – what you won't do.

To get it to help change work, ask the stubborn part if it will put the old, unwanted habit on the list of things it definitely won't do – the taboos, the no-nos if you like. If it agrees to the benefit of that person, change (other things being equal) almost always occurs. Unless someone's needs aren't met.

You could just ask it – 'Stubborn part thanks for doing what you did, can you now stubbornly do something more healthy and beneficial for this person for all the appropriate reasons?'

With lesser problems that might work too in

conjunction with some other stuff. I'm throwing out trouble-shooting ideas here folks to stimulate your own thought of what you *could* do.

Why you should thank your subconscious now and again.

Your subconscious does almost everything for you without one jot of gratitude from your conscious self. Ever thanked it? Even once? In order to get better rapport from the subconscious just say in your own mind every now and again, 'Thank you subconscious.' Don't be too surprised if you find yourself unconsciously smiling! One woman said to me, 'You talk about it as though it's a separate thing.' I said, 'It is.' I suspect though cannot prove that we are so dissociated from our deeper self by the modern birthing process which is highly abnormal.

How to ask your subconscious questions.

If you want to ask your subconscious yes/no questions you can do so in the following manner. All you need is a piece of string and a paper clip. The principle behind this technique is – ***the subconscious knows more about you than consciousness does.*** You have no idea how true this is.

- Tie the paper clip to the end of the string – this is your communication device.

- Rest one arm on the same side leg in a sitting position. Dangle the string and paper clip device from your first finger and thumb. Allow the device to rest.

- Say in your own mind, *'Subconscious I want to ask you some yes/no questions. Can you make the paper clip swing forward and back for yes and side to side for no?'*

- Ask away: keep questions simple, e.g. 'Do I have a phobia of phobias?' This gets you a yes/no response. Don't ask it weird occultic s**t or how to predict the future. Or if you do don't blame me for the info you get or the consequences thereof. I have asked my subconscious if I was allergic to something and it said no. It turned out to be right. However I have very good rapport with my subconscious: do you?

- **Warning:** *do not blame the Rogue Hypnotist because you claim he informed/told you how to do the above and you did it and it led to a serious problem – health or otherwise. What you do with this information is **YOUR** responsibility. Do nothing that possible endangers the health of yourself or others. I have much more knowledge about how the mind really works than most people. You don't yet have that knowledge.*

How to 'cure' mild unwanted feeling states/problems with a piece of string with something on the end.

Say you are at a party. Someone asks for some hypnosis for entertainment: try this – just ask for a piece of sewing thread and a paper clip – this is your 'hypno-pendulum.' Ask if anyone has a situation in which they feel mild nervousness or anxiety they'd like to be rid of in a specific situation. *You do NOT want to deal with bigger stuff.* Give the volunteer the makeshift hypno-pendulum, ask for silence and ask them to close their eyes as they stand or sit. Your hypnotic intent and the mysterious power of expectation will make this work...

String and paper clip change script.

Step 1: establish yes/no signals.

'Ok, just focus on your breathing...

just notice it...

in

and out...

don't try to change it...

(Allow them time to focus.)

Good...

Imagine *the thing you're holding*

is a magic hypno-pendulum...

Just let it hang from your finger and thumb...

That's it...

Don't do anything consciously...

but

focus on imagining *it moving forward and back...*

This is like nodding your head. You see?

It's an **affirmative**

...the **positive path** *in life,*

it's the **best thing** *to do.*

This is your **yes** *signal...*

(Wait till it happens.)

Excellent! (Verbal reward.)

The opposite is side to side.

It's a no.

It's a shaking of the head.

Like babies do

when they turn their head when they refuse food... (Idea seeding through analogy.)

So this time...

imagine that hypno-pendulum swaying side to side...

That's right.

This is your no signal.

(Don't emphasise the 'no' so much. It's a throwaway line. Wait for movement.)

Good.

Now clear your mind...

and let that pendulum rest...

(Stop it yourself if needed.)

Step 2: change work.

Now think of a time in your life

*in which you had some kind of **emotional response** (etc.)*

*you'd like to **change now...***

So, can you let me know...

unconsciously moving it...

or imagining moving it back and forth

*to indicate your **yes signal please...***

(Pause for signal)

Great!

Just imagine that in your mind;

*Not knowing know how **<u>you're</u> able to do this.***

(Say 'you're' as if addressing the *subconscious* only.)

*Not needing to know how **<u>you</u> are able to do this,*** *making that **change**,*

you don't and won't know...

*no idea how **this is possible**,*

right now,

*to **make that desired change...***

yet only in a way that

your subconscious feels is precisely,

pleasantly,

safely right for you...

Nothing for you to do at all,

*just **focus in on your breathing***

in and out

in and out...

and just allow yourself to know

really know, that...

the subconscious can change the intensity of that feeling

dramatically, right now!

Your subconscious can let you know

*when **that's occurred...***

*and as that **unconscious change somehow happens, now...***

*that changing part can communicate **YES!***

(Wait.)

*So if 0 is **no problem whatsoever** – how much better do you feel?'*

(*Troubleshooting tips:* If you like, before you change the feeling you can you can get the person to rate it on the 'S.U.D' - Standard Units of Distress - scale in their mind; this makes it more real/objective for some people. **Also note: when you get people to use the S.U.D you will immediately calm people and cause a pattern interrupt. Why? Because if you are thinking about rating an emotion/feeling you aren't feeling about it you are *thinking* about it. This will cause the emotion to be lessened all by itself.** If the feeling isn't completely better on completion of the above script but is lower in general ask the person if they want to take it down more using the pendulum for yes. If yes repeat change work step till all gone or until no more change occurs. I used to do this sort of things in pubs with friends when I first qualified as a hypnotherapist. Haven't done it in a while: now I act more 'mysteriously' and don't dish out the free hypnosis so readily. This creates the illusion that you are really holding back some _real_ 'power.' Final tip: if an abreaction develops use the method I outlined in book 1 to stop it.)

A helpful deepener: hypnotic blackboards.

As I learnt about hypnosis I realised that things, symbols related to school seemed common in change work, inductions etc. Perhaps they are simply examples of early learning sets described elsewhere in your book. Blackboards seem a favourite with many hypnotists. I have the first blackboard deepener for you here.

3 words in chalk deepener.

(Hypnosis is assumed)

'Imagine that you are in a hypnotic school.

That's it...

Walk down a corridor in this place of learning (places in the mind pattern see book 3, 'Powerful hypnosis')

and enter a wonderful classroom.

see a blackboard with chalk...

walk over and know

at a very deep level

that in a bit

you are going to write three appropriate words

on that blackboard...

one after the other...

and each time you write one

you go even deeper *than you just were...*

feeling more mesmerised, entranced and wonderful...

As and after you write it...

and by the time you've reached the third deeply hypnotic word...

you will have entered just the right level of

deep...hypnotic...trance, now

for you to achieve

all that you need

from this mightily hypnotic session...

Ok when I say 'now'

write the first hypnotic word

in that hypnotic chalk

that takes you deeper...

NOW!

(Pause for 10 seconds to allow this.)

Ok now you **feel that much deeper...**
(ambiguous)

it's almost time...to write your second word,
(variant of 'in a moment pattern')

maybe using different coloured chalk

it's up to you...

this is your experience...

Ok, ready to write the next word?

Here we go...and... ('and + pause' creates 'a
moment of hypnotic expectation')

NOW!

(Pause to allow processing time.)

You go that much deeper, *didn't you?*

Excellent!

You're doing wonderfully!

And one last time for luck...

Not yet but soon on the cue word...

choose a word that is SO powerfully hypnotic to YOU

that it takes you

to a very deep

peaceful...

changeful...

level of...

wonderful, blissful trance...

wonderful, blissful hypnosis...

NOW!!!!

(Allow processing time, 10 secs or so.)

Great!

Just enjoy that deep level of trance and hypnosis:

it can **feel wonderful** *doesn't it?!'*

(This works well because it uses the client's own subconscious symbols – namely certain subjective words that they will associate with going deeper – their own 'keys to the mind.')

See the appendix for a free bonus blackboard deepener!

Trauma trance: how to stop bleeding and other strange tricks with hypnosis.

Let's say someone has had an accident and they are bleeding; if this requires medical treatment then without doubt the person will be suggestible to helpful remedial action; it may be a 'survival trance' – the brain becomes highly motivated to take perceived authoritative advice to facilitate healing: anything will do!

Reframe trauma.

'That's a lot of good red healthy blood you have.'

This is an immediate pattern interrupt. *You* need to stay calm and keep you s**t together for it to work; if you scream and say it, well, it might not be SO effective! With children's scrapes etc. you can say stuff like,

*'It will go on bleeding a while but **relax** soon it will stop.'*

In this you are pacing their ongoing reality but then you tag on the conversational suggestion – it will stop.

In more severe cases you want to embed the following...

- **Stop (that) bleeding.**

- **ALLOW IT! DO IT! PERFORM THIS TASK!** (Use just one option.)

- **Let it happen now. Do this immediately. Right now, etc.**

Reframe/pattern interrupt.

*'When would you like to **stop bleeding, now** or a bit later?'*

Or

'Would you like to stop bleeding? Now, has anyone asked you this yet?

Or

*'Did you know it's possible to **stop bleeding, now?'***

This will probably confuse someone somewhat. A good thing.

Waking suggestions through framing/priming and truism.

*'Everyone controls their bleeding – it's a thing your unconscious does for you. When you cut your knee as a child you could **stop the bleeding.** You don't **allow it** consciously. Your heart rate slows right down as you calm down but another part of you does that so just **let this occur,** now.'*

In this short paragraph you will,

- Embed commands in the highly suggestible trauma trance.

- State truisms which lower the conscious mind's analytical guard.

- Prime unconscious responses by referring to times when everyone knows blood flow is altered.

You can when faced with a trauma trance lie and say,

- 'I'm a doctor; look at me – you'll be fine.'

That in itself will marshal a healing response.

The stress levels will plummet enabling a lessened pain response and a better healing response. Stress interferes with healing AND makes injuries more painful. If you are uncomfortable with lying you can grow up and think, 'Oh well it's to help someone else,' or you can say, 'I have seen this before; you'll recover my sister/monkey etc. had the same problem and was fine.'

- Get them to fixate on you – either eye contact, touch etc. A great trick to relax a distressed person is to place a slightly tense hand on a shoulder and then slowly relax it – this is a non-verbal suggestion to relax. It works and feels nice.

- Give immediate waking suggestions that are the opposite of their unpleasant and ongoing reality.

'That burning **sensations can change** to a cooling one and spread across your whole body etc.'

'That pain can quickly become less of a problem as **you feel more**

comfortable etc.'

You will obviously have to elaborate on these and keep talking and making healing suggestions up on the fly, off the cuff: trust your subconscious to aid you. It will.

- Future pace: get the person to imagine a time in the future when they are 'all better.' This will motivate 'healing responses.'

Some medical professionals reading this will think: 'I won't install 'false hope' in my patients!' Ok smart arse but you're ok suggesting 'certain despair' are you???! Remember voodoo deaths - if you believe, it can happen. Interestingly between 80-90% of oncologists (Cancer docs) won't use chemotherapy etc. if THEY get cancer. Hmmmm?

How to make a woman's entire body orgasmic.

Woman have orgasmic potential all over their body. Men don't; just as well or nothing would get done. With this in mind knowing that the unconscious knows this is true, no matter what consciousness thinks it knows I have written this script for those who might be interested. It may have serious applications beyond the kinkily obvious. I adapted this from a treatment that Milton Erickson devised for a lady who was disabled, believed she'd never orgasm and feared she'd never meet the man of her dreams. Dr. Erickson swiftly proved her wrong!

'Orgasmic body.'

(Hypnosis of one kind or another assumed)

'What if I told you that you have erectile tissue in many places?

Your unconscious knows this is true...

no matter what the other part thinks it believes...

You thought perhaps it was just down there...

Just that place?

No.

When it's bitterly cold outside your nose hardened.

If you flick your nipple it will harden.

*Ever had a great kiss that let you top lip be**come** thick and warm?*

So many parts of you are interconnected...

In ways you don't know but <u>YOU</u> do... (the second you being the unconscious)

all your sexual feelings are connected to all your other feelings.

At just the right time many parts of you can **be simultaneously aroused and sensitive.**

How would it feel if the sexiest man you've ever met touched your breast?

Would you **feel hot and bothered?**

Would you blush?

Feel embarrassed? (She may flush somewhere around here!)

Or all and both?

Would you get that deep red flush from that touch?

Some woman can feel amazing sensations from a handshake...

with just the right man of course.

You unconsciously realise this is true

but you've always known deep inside...

Every young lady can recall her first kiss with her first true love...

Have you had a better orgasm?

Could there be one?

The curl of a tongue around a nipple.

You felt the sucking...the searching, did you not?

Enjoyed that exploration of your entire body...

to see...

find out...

discover...

what really turns you on...

and where...

Not just <u>there</u>... (guess where <u>there</u> is?)

but in many places that will...

surprise and delight you...

at just the right time...

in any appropriate place...

or position...

with just the right person...

*to **feel** that **amazingly sensitive** too...*

Is your curiosity of the possibilities

of these enticing ideas, these hypnotic realities

that can become your reality

aroused?

Being born a woman is a gift

because you were created

with more **pleasure** *potential...*

with **intense feelings**

more and more and more, now...

and a woman can **have multiple orgasms**

from many sources of stimulation...

than a man can...

but the secret is:

a man can make all that happen...

Did you **feel those shivers**

go up and down your neck

when he kissed it?

Or maybe it was your whole spine that tingled?

You **know those naughty tingles?**

Perhaps you **feel those butterflies** *in your tummy...*

That **excited** *delightful nervousness...*

That irrational **warmth...**

You know all these feelings deep inside...

Consider these ideas at a very deep level...

so that you make them your own...

somehow...

in your own unique way...

as the special lady that you are, now...

enjoy the delight of the discovery...

Imagine that...

the seeds have been planted...

I wonder if you wonder...

what pleasures you will succumb to?'

(If this needs any explanation – see me after class.)

How to create the hypnotic mood.

You can just talk about hypnosis and what it does for people, just discussing it with the future hypnotee will start 'moving things' for them at a subconscious level; seeding ideas of what is possible, telling them about others who have benefitted. I once booked a session over the phone with an insomnia client and she slept well that night. I hadn't even seen her yet!!! As a result of this she said, 'You must be good!' You can tell them simply what the subconscious does for them: doing so is hypnotic and it starts to create conscious/subconscious dissociation discussed in book 2, 'Mastering hypnotic language,' with a script provided: here is another way to do it.

What your subconscious does for you.

(Hypnosis, conversational, waking: up to you)

'There's a known function of mind that does its own thing...

it doesn't matter what you think or consciously believe...

that part notices things that consciousness

doesn't...

like changing voice tones...

it dreams dreams while **you sleep comfortably**

...it knows how to do many things on your behalf...

Its prime directive is to keep you alive...

It's in charge off all your emotions...

it grows nails...

it salivates at the sight of tasty food...

it is the place where laughter comes from...

it controls your startle response...

it controls that knee reflex you get when a doctor taps that place with a little hammer...

it knows exactly how to allow you to **calm down...**

processes nutrients from what you take in...

it protects your eyes from dust...

it sheds skin cells...

old ideas...

it already knows how to **go into trance...**

it grows hair...

it fights germs, infections...

in can heal you, unconsciously...

so many processes outside of awareness...

that it can attend to...

without needing any part of that other part's interference...

it sighs for you...

it breathes easily *for you*

all beyond your conscious awareness...

It knows all about you...

all...about...you...

it is your wiser self...

your/re unconscious...

some people call it...

but it doesn't care what labels...

what metaphors

merely approximate its manifold capacities...

because it does so many helpful things for you...

each and both of you, regardless...

so just **relax**

and **take it easy**

it kind of dreams during the day too...

when **just the right mood takes it...**

It controls so many mind-body processes on your behalf...

too many to list here...

like the staff of a hotel...

behind the scenes...

keeping the whole thing

running **smoothly.**

And when a hypnotist helps you **enter your own trance...**

you'll find that's the only part that need **listen.'**

All hypnotists are trying to pry open 'the window of influence' when the conscious guard goes down and the door to the 'deeper-self' opens. Guards are looking out for danger; when no danger presents itself they lower the drawbridge.

What is hypnotic intent?

It's a bit like being the bullfighter knowing 'bullnosis'; you have your bag of tricks and you await an 'opening' in the client's subconscious which you actively create through your knowledge base and skills. Your hypnotic intent is knowing with 100% certainty that whoever you are hypnotising – 'Your a*s/a**e is mine!'

How to create therapeutic embeds.

Embedded commands are hidden commands, that is - *direct suggestions* hiding within more 'permissive' style hypnotic language. This is very easy; it has been covered somewhat if you noticed in book 3 with the Total Confidence Boost script. You simply embed what you want the subconscious to do within the wider context of the trance languaging you are using. Tell the subconscious in no uncertain terms what to do: this is why embeds are covert because they bypass conscious awareness, unless you are looking out for them and even so they can still work on you or against you. Some examples follow.

You have full self-belief.

Control your portion size.

Leave those nails alone.

Feel more energy.

You feel so much calmer.

Your mood improves.

Imagine a brighter future.

You blood pressure lowers.

That face relaxes easily.

Your unconscious makes an association.

Ignore certain inappropriate urges.

You feel so happy.

No discomfort.

Pay attention to that signal.

Learn easily.

Alter that response.

Move beyond that.

Get rid of that unhealthy smoking habit.

Eliminate that habit, now.

Be completely free from x (habit etc.)

Adopt some new ideas.

Change those former assumptions.

Think about things differently.

Focus laser-like on your goals.

Enjoy the intensity of that focus.

Observe it from the outside.

Just keep improving.

Notice yourself responding differently.

Let those wonderful feelings flow through you.

Achieve your goals.

See the funny side.

See the bigger picture.

That compulsion diminishes.

Change at a deep level.

Ignore the irrelevant when you x (play a sport etc.)

All contain verbs of one kind or another because you are telling the subconscious what to do – you are 'directionalising' it.

How to avoid being hypnotised.

Ormond McGill the world famous American hypnotist claimed that by pressing your tongue on the roof of your mouth and thus preventing 'sub-vocalisation' you could prevent hypnosis occurring. I say if you feel you are being hypnotised against your will, if you feel oddly trancey and suddenly become aware of it – *get out of that environment and away from that person fast!* Unwanted hypnosis is a form of assault as far as I am concerned.

NOTE:
SUGGESTIBILTY/PROGRAMABILITY CAN BE INCREAESED RAPIDLY AND MARKEDLY BY A QUICK AND DRAMATIC ALTERATION IN ENVIRONMENT OR TO IT.

The tremblingly alive mind: why brainwashing 'con-versions' occur!

In a word: stress! If you can find a person's weak spot and attack it/exploit it you can help trigger the ***physiological*** responses that leads to conversions: religious, political, cultic. The discovery Of Winston Smith's fear of rats is utilised to make him 'love Big Brother' by O'Brien in 1984. Of course he has been tortured through starvation, beatings and electrocution to the brain. **The aim: unrelenting tension and excitation until suggestibility is increased and total submission fully occurs.**

Interrogators in dictatorships and elsewhere search for 'sensitive topics' and play on these until confession occurs. The process is similar to breaking a horse. Once perceived as the only escape from the continuing stressor, submission to obedience is willingly sought by the victim hoping for peace. Even in democracies police will use such tactics if convinced a suspect is guilty and force a wrongful confession from an innocent person. This has even been done to children/minors.

If the interrogator fails to locate suitable past 'guilts' or 'anxieties' to work upon and press he will use *interpretation (a form of suggestion/implication) and a twisting of facts* to achieve his end. A similar process occurs in psycho-analysis. Some doctors used such methods on World War Two veterans to 'cure' PTSD.

The excitation reaches a peak, a psychological 'breaking point.' At this moment all the suggestions are accepted ***physiologically:*** a state of absolute calm follows and the new beliefs are firmly rooted in the victim. Thus are men and women's minds raped.

Gradual criticism: the North Korean's technique to create a 'Manchurian candidate.'

Some US Army etc. POWs were brainwashed by the Communist North Koreans during the Korean war. How? Well to describe all the methodologies would require a whole book in itself. This was one method the Commie bar-stewards favoured...

- Take one patriotic GI.

- Get him to admit to/write down one thing about his country he isn't 100% happy with.

- Over time get him to write a whole list of things.

- Focus his mind solely on the 'bad side' of his country.

- At the same time start indoctrination as to how Commie-land has none of these problems etc.

In other words you change their minds gradually, through criticism. However 99.9% of the brainwashing broke down as soon as the US troops returned home. Why? **They were no longer in a controlled cult environment so the brain auto-corrected itself.** It is also possible many were faking successful 'indoctrination' to avoid punishment and so survive capture.

How to do the 'hypnotic stare' - properly.

This is how you do the hypnotic stare, no words are needed:

- Look into your victim's eyes.

- With your two first fingers (think a 'V' sign or 'up yours' if you're English), point them at the eyes of your victim. Not in them!

- Then turn your fingers from their eyes toward yours. As if saying by gesture – '...look into my eyes.'

- Rest your hand.

- As you look into their eyes imagine that you are looking 'through' them. Say at a point about two to three inches behind their eyes – almost as if you are staring through the eyes to the subconscious/unconscious.

- When the victim's eyes look glassy, spacey, trancey begin your rapid induction procedure or just say, 'Close your eyes...' and do whatever you want to induce hypnotic trance.

How cults capture minds!

Well for a start:

- 'Flirty fishing' – using very attractive cult members to 'lure' unsuspecting saps in with the illusion of having sex with the 'flirty fisher.' My friend was once approached by two 16 year old cute blonde girl cultists who tried to ensnare him while he was out shopping alone one lunchtime. Unfortunately for them he was 'crazier' than they were and he freaked them out so they soon left him alone! Some Jehovah's Witnesses were lurking around my area not a long while back, they had brought with them an incredibly attractive blonde woman. I mean she was a knock-out; I was half-tempted to convert!!!

- If you are ever with a cultist or in a cultic environment eat and drink nothing offered. It could be drugged.

Who do cults look for?

Losers, weirdoes right? Wrong. They look for

these traits in 'recruits':

1. The 'economically sound'; all the better to be robbed.

2. Has average to above average intelligence; more suggestible.

3. Has a good education; more suggestible. Remember the Nazi party members tended to be the well-educated, lower middle classes – not the Neo-Nazi morons of today. In fact doctors were the biggest professional group in the Nazi party.

4. Is *'idealistic.'* (Gullible, naïve, sucker!)

What is a cult precisely?

We all kind of 'know' intuitively but there is a working 'definition' according to several different researchers. Psychological coercion must be used in recruiting/indoctrinating possible members. Cult identifiers include:

- Elitism.

- Its 'originator' and first leader is: self-appointed, dogmatic, messianic, unaccountable, 'charismatic.' Ahem, sound familiar?

- 'End justifies the means' mentality for funding or recruitment.

- Wealth accrued benefits leaders and NOT members.

To a certain extent this sounds like EVERY civilised country on earth!!!

Some researchers claim there are broadly speaking 2 major forms of cults: Pseudo 'religious' and 'therapeutic.' Other researchers don't but I use the term 'pseudo' because religions and therapy are not always bad.

Pseudo 'Religious' cults:

- Communal living.

- Cultists do not work in wider society.

- Recruits ensnared in early 20s.

- Registered as: 'religious groups.'

- Claim to offer association with an organisation: wanting to 'make the world a better place' through political, spiritual means etc.

- Nazism and communism are 'secular' political cults but none the less 'religious' for that. In such societies God = the State.

Pseudo 'Therapy' cults:

- Rarely communal.

- Members work in wider world.

- Recruitment age = mid 30s. This is the age when lots of people start thinking, 'Where is my life going?'

- Registered as: 'not for profit' groups.

- Claim to offer association with a group giving courses in some kind of 'self-improvement' or 'self-help' technique or 'therapy.'

Does NLP fit this? Does psychoanalysis? Technically, in many ways I think they do. So do lots of other 'human potential' movement courses and teaching etc. We will briefly examine the methodologies of one sub type of pseudo therapy cult – the 'Commercial Cult.'

The 'Commercial Cult.'

Cults that promise commercial gain as their base are labelled by some researchers as 'cults of greed.'

- Does this sound familiar? Follow our 'special programme for success' and you *will* become very rich!

- The cult leader is the role model - do what he or she says then you will be successful too. Think of any wildly popular self-help courses like this?

- Mind control = you pay for an interminable mountain of 'motivational' resources which reveal the secrets of success – tapes and videos (formerly), CDs and DVDs books, seminars all of which are claimed to help you 'succeed!' The internet is filled with bunkum like this; think of any world famous teacher of 'success secrets' – they differ how?! How many 'hypnotherapists' offer this sort of dross! *Of course some are well-*

intentioned and produce good self-help material, they have integrity and are genuinely seeking to help people but beware of the many crooks! Psychopaths don't carry axes: they wear suits!

- Reality check: the products themselves create the cult's **mind control environment;** brainwashing you into believing in the delusions of 'success.'

- Recruits volunteer slave labour in the hope of that one trick or gimmick that will *'give you the edge.'* Of course the cult organisation fails to admit the main way the cult leaders make their crispy cash is by selling 'motivation material' to the suckers! ***Ponzi schemes of the mind!***

All 'civilised' societies are designed so only a **few** live high on the hog. Got it? Doesn't mean you can't succeed but you have to do it using your own brains and hard work: that's reality. If you don't have connections or money it's going to be harder and take longer time (probably).

Cults and their methods will be more extensively covered in book 5, 'Wizards of trance.' This book offers but a taster.

Insidious methodologies of cultic indoctrination:

I am also going to indicate where 'cultic strategies' are used in wider society. Although they are all interconnected these 8 level methodologies include:

1. **Idea programming.**

2. **Breaking down the body.**

3. **Emotional overload.**

4. **Exploiting the herd instinct.**

5. **Controlling universal human needs.**

6. **Infantilisation.**

7. **Breaking taboos.**

8. **Acceptance of hierarchy.**

Level 1: Idea programming through trance/suggestion processes.

Hypnosis: obviously, sadly but as you have seen (especially if you've read all my books!) waking hypnosis is used in much of wider society. Hypnosis and hypnoidal states can be induced by 'relaxation' or 'meditation.' Cults know this: infamous 'Jonestown' cult leader Jim Jones induced hypnosis in his slaves 4 times a day through PMR (Progressive Muscle Relaxation), making them hyper-programmable.

Warping of time sense: TV, boring or stressful work. Clocks, watches are often removed by cults – producing a 'timeless feeling' - like in hypnosis folks! Nothing that you experience can therefore be differentiated according to time. You are deprived of all ways of measuring time basically.

Confusing doctrines that make no logical, provable sense: you could list many major world religions here which are riddled with internal inconsistencies, political campaigns and more. The point is *LOGIC AND REASONING ARE REJECTED.* This generalises as a principle of living. Confusion is hypnotic; only the 'wise elders' may interpret 'the revelation.'

Speaking with forked tongue – 'Metacommunication': is a secondary communication, including indirect cues, about how any information is meant to be interpreted. Basically saying one thing and meaning another or communicating multi-level messages. Well this exists in many contexts including 'seduction hypnosis,' 'erotic literature' etc., even the news! This technique also includes implanting **subliminal messages** through key words or phrases (embeds!) in overly long (fatigue) and confusing monologues. **Live NLP courses all use this principle.** I don't know one that doesn't do this!

Chanting away thought: all major religions use this. TM uses it 'internally' – mantras. Focus of attention solely on cultic ideas etc. Even football (soccer) crowds do this at matches.

Level 2: Breaking down the body to break down the mind.

No rest for the wicked - sleep deprivation: this causes anxiety, depression, madness and breaking point; it also makes you suggestible and unable to resist coercion. A bad workplace or home situation can engender this. Sleep problems = exhaustion and both are causes of depression.

Dietary modification: going on a 'get slim' diet, low carbs etc. Religious fasting. This breaks down resistance to mind control. The nervous system is deprived of nutrients and is far too weak to resist and marshal psychological defences.

Level 3: Tipping over the edge - emotional overload.

Thou shalt feel guilt!: 'So and so is starving!' 'There are only x amount of wombats: have you no heart???! Give us your money!' - a.k.a: various charities' ad campaigns. 'Sins' must be purged for 'salvation'!!!! Of course the 'sins' of the former way of living must be believed to be catastrophic for conversation to occur.

Fear is the mind killer: advertising, politics, if you don't tidy your room! Cults issue physical threats for disobedience, this includes murder. Cults are just like crime syndicates.

The constant activation of 'fight or flight' eventually causes heightened emotional arousal which leads to 'black and white thinking.'

Calculated verbal Abuse: where the f**k do we start here!!! Army, school, home, a relationship, while driving a car etc. Cultists can be desensitised to abuse and foul language so seeing it as normal, acceptable: also they become stiffened to 'attack' by 'outsiders.'

It's confession time!: breaking sense of self-esteem, self-worth, ahem - try a woman's magazine! The aim? Annihilation of a solid sense of self through confession of perceived/interpreted weaknesses and deepest feelings of doubt, guilt, anxiety etc. Sound familiar?

Breaking the beast of burden sessions: a lone or perhaps several cult members and leaders *attack the character of another person mercilessly,* sometimes for hours and hours on end without rest. Cults will not stop these sessions until their victim is crying uncontrollably. These techniques are used by the Chinese Communists, in acting training and many other non-cult environments: how about schools? Some people's families do this. Psycho-analysis does this, in fact Freud resented the Sabbath as a day of rest because it gave his 'patients' time to rest!!! He wanted access to them 7 days a week.

I am reminded of a stable I visited; there was a beautiful black stallion locked up in a lone stall. He was angry, wild and snorted at anyone who got too close. I asked one of the stable girls why he was locked up and chained. I was given some B-S about him not being a 'nice horse' etc. I knew it wasn't true. He was a prince of horses and no one could break him. That's why he was locked up – he had unbreakable spirit.

Level 4: People into sheeple - exploiting the herd instinct.

Not so splendid isolation: in any social group, non-group-think members are given the 'cold shoulder,' 'sent to Coventry.' Sense of reality, connectedness, logic and 'other opinion' impossible. Your emotional need for intimacy cannot be met.

Crowding out choice with peer pressure:
when isn't peer pressure involved? Especially
when we are in our teens. Personal doubt and
resistance to 'new ideas' is squashed by
exploiting the 'tribal need.' See book 3 for
more on this. *Most people are sheep – they
follow the herd despite their own reservations.*
Much social psychology research has been
done on this in various questionable studies.

Strategic 'finger pointing': a.k.a: the
blame game. In wider society lots of groups
are 'blamed' for things they didn't do. You are
responsible yet not responsible: doublethink.

Push me pull you controlled approval:
operant conditioning used in homes, schools,
workplace etc. Rewarding and punishing
(interchangeably/arbitrarily) for *the same
actions.* This produces complete confusion,
vulnerability and total dependence. This is
what child abusers do to their victims.

**Level 5: Controlling universal human
needs.**

'Love Bombing': at least 1 world famous
fast food chain uses this as a 'human

management' tool. Cults create a faux family, and so seem to fulfil the need for attention – this can be achieved through hugging, kissing, touching and most importantly flattery: the verbal hug. Ever noticed close families 'verbally groom' one another by saying things like, 'I like that new outfit, top, hairstyle etc.' This is the human equivalent of eating each other's mites in primates.

Removal of your privacy: this occurs most obviously in prison, at school, in the workplace; you have supervisors. NSA spying???! CCTV cameras which are ALL OVER THE PLACE in England. You have no THOUGHT TIME to ruminate/contemplate about what is going on and so your rational brain is given no space to 'kick in.' We all need some quiet contemplation time to avoid stress and ponder things. Cult 'recruits' remain immersed in the group of true-believers.

Relationship replacement: the cult breaks all old links and creates new ones. Ending of emotional needs via close and intimate relationships happen when people leave home and go to college/University, when we emigrate or relocate for a new job. Old ties are destroyed, new cult family/marriage is essential to 'integration.'

Overwhelming financial commitment: general taxation??! In the middle ages the Catholic Church demanded 'Peter's Pence.' Produces? Dependence dummy! Bridges are burnt – interdependence with cult? Total.

Level 6: Creating 'kidults' - infantilisation.

'Disinhibition': sensitivity training, acting training (same things.) ***Child-like behaviour in adults produces child-like obedience.*** Many acting schools want this in actors so directors can bully them around etc.

Mad 'games': goal? *Infantilisation.* Actors play various 'games' during their training especially Lee Strasbourg, Stanislavski type training. Obscure rules employed = looking to group leaders for answers about everything.

Level 7: Creating 'new normals' - breaking taboos.

Total annihilation of 'old values': the 1930s, 1960s, porn 'stars.' 'Old' traditions are condemned regularly. 'New' life and values are praised. Carrot and stick: simple. In acting schools male actors are told to 'rape' female actors, both sexes are encouraged to strip off and roll around on the floor touching one another. These were techniques used in 'Sensitivity Training.'

Level 8: Loving Big Brother* – acceptance of the hierarchy.

Rigid, inflexible rules: an inflexible management style? At least one major UK retailer uses this: fact. A.k.a - bullying????! Eating, going to the toilet, taking needed medical treatments are ALL regulated by the cult – like a pseudo mummy and daddy. Basically you can't take a p**s without permission. *Some call centres in the UK use this as 'normal' operating procedure.*

Strict dress codes: all armed forces and police. School uniform is worn by all children in the UK up until 16 years old: it is compulsory. This de-individuates the child: *'uni-form' – 'one form.'* In medieval England there were laws preventing peasants who prospered from dressing like their 'betters.' It was one of the causes of peasants' revolts across Europe following mass depopulation and so higher wages/better negotiating conditions caused by the Black Death. What about a nightclub? They have dress codes. Religious and social hierarchies historically wear strange 'wizard outfits' and contemporaneously: can you afford an expensive suit???

'Ornate' hierarchy: Forbes magazine, Tatler Magazine, the Oscars etc. To flaunt is to 'display oneself conspicuously, defiantly, or boldly' (in public) and 'to parade or display ostentatiously.' Celebs, royalty – where do we start!

No questions: the workplace, home, religious dogma, science, TV, politicians etc. Orderz vich must be obeyed! ONLY 'POSITIVE' THINKING ALLOWED! Happy, happy faces people! 'All is for the best in all possible worlds!' as Dr. Pangloss says in Candide.

Did you know the term 'Big Brother' is derived from the bureaucratic training schools of ancient Sumer. 'Big Brother' was the name given to the class tutor

REMEMBER: BREAKING DOWN ONLY WORKS IF YOU <u>ACCEPT THE AUTHORITY OF THE PERSON ATTACKING YOU.</u> IF YOU REJECT IT AND SEE THE PERSON AS A LOON OR IDIOT OR EVIL YOU CAN RETAIN YOUR MENTAL FACULTIES. REMAIN CALM, HAVE A SENSE OF HUMOUR.

The aim of all this evil crap? As said before - pressure continues to a 'breaking point,' that is physical and mental breakdown, making one ***highly vulnerable to suggestion as critical ability is severely impaired in such a hyper-aroused state.*** This is soon accompanied by a *sudden* personality change; for the worse, as all the programming suddenly 'takes' – a mind control slave has been created. Sounds like starting a new job!

Ok that's the basic story for beginners. As I said earlier, I think all these characteristics are found to a lesser or greater degrees in many places, situations, relationships in wider society. In a cult the purpose is to create *__a human robot__*.

So you have the knowledge. Let's say you are evil, bat s**t crazy and want to form your own cult. How do you go about ensuring your demented quest becomes a reality?

How to form a cult for the deranged control freak.

- **Be a psychopath:** or a group of them: this is essential.

- **Create a pseudo society:** an inversion of a real one.

- **Make up a history of the world.**

- **Offer people secret knowledge:** of success, money, spiritual fulfilment etc.

- **Offer people the illusion of fake security and stability**: through a rigid hierarchy and belief system. If you can convince the women they can have 'security' you can take over an entire society.

- **Teach cultists an 'us and them' mentality:** unbelievers and believers are two separate 'species.' Without the potential for conflict and a pseudo sense of higher self-importance from belonging to 'the club,' cults would fail.

- **Take cult member children and condition them**: as early as possible.

- **Use highly suggestible and attractive women/men**: to lure in men and women recruits.

- **Systematically employ scientific mind control strategies:** hypnosis, drugs, isolation, behaviourism, mantras and slogans at the least to brainwash people.

- **Have a BIG BROTHER leader:** he knows all and cares about all IF they do exactly as he says. Otherwise: imagine someone evil drawing their finger across their neck as they look at you!

- **Feed off of a dominant culture**: in decline.

- **Demand fanatical devotion**: and enforce through ostentatious rewards and extreme punishments.

- **Create an inner circle of 'adepts':** who have the 'true knowledge.' Lie to the underlings that 'goodthinking' will lead to access to this inner circle. But make sure it never _really_ happens.

- **Conflicting exoteric/esoteric agenda:** profess a public exoteric agenda of desiring 'world peace' etc. but have a secret esoteric agenda only know to adepts of tyrannical 'world domination.' All cults are 'globalists.'

- **Use the cultic principle of 'plausible continuity':** this is a fancy term for good old 'pacing and leading.' I told you NLP predates the

70s because this stuff is OLD. So what is 'PC'? You take an existing belief system and add to it, develop it, claim 'new revelations' that build on the old. Thus giving the new cult faux respectability by being an offshoot of another more 'reputable' one.

- **Separation of place and environment:** you must keep cult members isolated for extensive periods of time. Not solitary confinement – though that is used in brainwashing but isolation with the group believers so that you are 'immersed' in cult-think. No other beliefs are permitted. Think Jim Jones island or North Korea. North Korea is a hereditary monarchy 'cult state.'

- **Inbreeding:** believers only breed with other believers. Simple. This ensures over time 'genetic differentiation' from the 'others' based not solely on attraction but on 'congruency of belief.' Cult babies may then be indoctrinated from birth: in a sociological 'Skinner's Box.'

- **Weird rites:** any cult worth its weight does weird s**t in mass groups, with chanting, outfits (at least for 'priests/priestesses' etc.) Think of Communist military parades.

- **Offers 'material transcendent purpose':** what the flip is this? In order to get people to act like moronic zombies <u>now</u> you must promise them 'salvation' or becoming part of an 'elect' <u>post death.</u> If your cult is 'secular' and none are even though some pretend to be – you must offer 'glory' in this life. Not your own but 'for the cause.'

- **Amass MASSIVE financial clout:** you must have LOTS of money to maintain a cult. There are no gurus in cardboard boxes! ***POWER = MONEY = POWER!***

- **Political clout:** over time you must start to get movers and shakers on board or on the payroll. Think of the Godfather films with Don Corleone buying politicians etc.

- **Offer a sense of pseudo 'belonging' to the excluded:** i.e. 'inclusivity.' The down and outs, the proles, the huddled masses, this group or that group that feels a stranger in a strange land; in effect - the powerless. In the insect like group there is 'belonging-ness' and vicarious 'power' through association with those who ARE powerful. 'Belonging' in this context actually means 'owned.'

- **Attack and destroy detractors if possible:** to protect the 'cult entity/corporation.' This is to show the 'life and death' power of the cult leaders to their own members primarily.

- **Normalise all abuse:** because all types of abuse are endemic in cults you MUST normalise it. It must be widespread so everyone experiences it. **IF everyone experiences it, it must be normal!**

- **Create a 'new morality':** you must, must, must create a new dispensation – a new law code, a new way of living, of relating to one another and it MUST be different from the 'outgroup.'

- **Illusion of power:** convince people they will have a share of the cult's power, in time: the so-called 'trickle down' effect in cult form.

- **Install doublethink:** convince cultists that slavery is freedom. This is also known as cognitive dissonance.

- **Create an 'end of the world scenario' that never happens:** this is like the donkey that tries to get the carrot that dangles off a stick, always an inch away from his being able to bite it.

- **Cultic reframing:** whatever happens: good or bad to the cult is as a result of 'cultic piety.' Low piety = punishment by the cosmos/the cults entity or familiar. ***Thus all failure is the member's fault.*** Giving money to the cult leader seems to 'atone' for this 'sin.'

- **Create 'angels' and 'demons':** cults often claim that a supernatural 'war' is ongoing between a 'dark' or 'light' side (whether this is actually true or not is immaterial) – the cult members almost always believe they are fighting with the forces of 'light.' *The exact opposite would seem to be true.*

- **Hate wider normal society:** a cult *must* be covertly wishing to destroy its host - the cult is merely the first vehicle in doing so. Think of secular 'cults,' Communism, Nazism etc. Both tolerated and what were the results in a moment of crisis? All cults MUST be crushed at birth. Why aren't they?

In summation: the main thing ideologically that makes a cult a cult is its aim is to -

- Install through **rapid** and **violently coercive means** of MIND CONTROL an **incredibly fictitious view of reality** in its members' heads causing actual **physiological personality change**: the human robot.

- To use the human robot as a source of **exploitation** and as a **tool of intrigue** for the cult hierarchy's nefarious ends.

The basic mechanics of brainwashing have been covered elsewhere in this book, to the degree that this is possible in a relatively brief tour. See 'Wizards of trance' for greater detail.

WARNING: Cult recruiters are not usually visually identifiable. They don't wear badges saying, 'cult recruiter.' They appear to be just regular people who appear to be <u>very friendly.</u>

<u>Anyone</u> can become a victim of cult techniques of

psychological coercion. *__The safest people seem to be the seriously mentally ill*!!! And those that know exactly how to spot a cult. Like YOU!__*

NEVER seek to infiltrate a cult: too damned dangerous!!!!

*Not so crazy after all. Just coz you ain't paranoid don't mean they ain't out to getcha.

How to make someone hypnotically deaf.

(Deep hypnosis assumed)

Only do this with talented hypnotic subjects with whom you have very good rapport/trust; not all clients are capable of such 'deep hypnotic phenomena.' If someone wishes to experience hypnotic deafness it can be this easy...

Hypnotic deafness script.

'When I count to 3 and say, 'Shhh!'

you will temporarily be hypnotically stone cold deaf...

(I say 'hypnotically' so they know it's not 'real' deafness, and so less likely to induce anxiety)

*but you'll **feel wonderfully relaxed and at peace with that***

brief spell of comforting silence...

knowing it will only be for such a short duration...

say only 5 seconds...

easy

...until I say 'bang!'...because a part of you can still hear...

(If you are worried they won't 'hear' your trigger, set up one whereby you touch their shoulder etc.)

and then your sense of hearing will instantly return...

*Ok, here/**hear** we **go**...* (embedded priming)

1-2-3 'shhh!'

(Pause for 5 seconds.)

'Bang!'

(Or touch them.)

Hearing back to normal feeling amazing!'

I have never found any reason to use this in hypnotherapy. It has been used by others in experimental hypnosis and some forms of 'therapy.' Be warned – get someone's permission first! **If you do this even with**

someone's permission it can produce terrible anxiety! That is why I have framed it as I have in the above script. Just because you know now how to do something doesn't mean you *ever* SHOULD!

<u>Note for the feint-hearted:</u> the person does <u>not</u> become stone cold deaf. As I said this is why I use the word 'hypnotically,' it is suggestive of a passing trick. A part of them can hear, it just isn't relaying sound through properly to 'awareness' – a bit like hypnotic pain control. We do this anyway when we concentrate, we forget/ignore outside noises consciously but the subconscious can hear them. *All hypnotic phenomena exists in waking conscious states now and again.* You can prime the subconscious to do this by getting subjects to remember the above times they may have ignored sounds totally or maybe when they had a blocked up ear from ear wax. Use anything similar – I will go into this properly in the next module. You can say, 'What would it be like to be deaf? Can you imagine?'

The above is a very simple method to create this very real hypnotic phenomena: there is also a more Ericksonian approach which I might teach you in a later book. **_As you can see hypnosis is capable of producing profound, even alarming physiological change._**

Hypno-party tricks: how to make someone forget their own name and other pointless nonsense.

You can do this in eyes shut hypnosis or waking; it's up to you. Sometimes it's as simple as getting them to look into your eyes or at a finger nail knuckle etc. (yours or theirs), to distract consciousness and then proceed with your patter. Practise makes perfect.

So how do you make this silly stuff *really* work?

The plan.

1. In setting **hypnotic context**: just say,

'I am a hypnotist,' matter of factly.

This starts up associational networks in the mind that you do 'weird s**t' to people! In our culture they've seen Derren Brown, Paul Mckenna stuff, you name it – so that's where you start. It puts people into altered states just saying that!

2. In order for hypnotic phenomena or hypnotic mind games to work you must get a

person to **re-associate to times they did something similar** – then it works. Remember from my other books (if you've read them) hypnosis utilises natural 're-association.'

You set up the subconscious by saying:

'You know that time you did x? Well mind trick y is like that.'

'You ever put your wallet/purse somewhere and couldn't remember where it was? Or did you ever get so distracted by something that **you forgot** *something you usually remember? Have you ever been introduced to someone new at a party or just starting a new job and someone else talks to you and* **you forgot that name.'**

Then the subconscious says, 'Oh I know, yeah I can do that.' You trigger a TDS – transderivational search. This is also idea seeding. You don't need to embed but you can add it if you want. Just another option.

3. The next part is that you symbolically, figuratively or descriptively **juice up the**

imagination somewhat...

'Can you imagine that I have it here in my hand as I reach over and take that name out...' (act as though you are taking it out of their mind.)

Or

'Can you just imagine your name is on a white/blackboard and you just wiped it out.'

Or

*'Imagine a place of forgetting in your mind. It's the place you put everything you forgot; maybe **your** socks, a person's **name** even if **you** only **forgot it** for a few seconds before you pulled it back out again.'*

(Instead of a place in the mind pattern you can say the 'book of forgetting.' Get them to imagine their name being placed in it. Or you could use a black box etc.)

At each stage of any hypnotic process you look for the moment of hypnotic surrender – the **'it's sunk in'** and been accepted moment.

NOTE: steps 2 and 3 can be reversed in order, experiment to see what works best.

4. Use of an 'in a moment' pattern variant followed by a direct and vivid description in no uncertain terms of what behaviour you want the victim/hypno-mind-slave to experience.

'Soon I'll count to 3 and click my fingers and you will have totally forgotten your name.'

5. Activate trigger:

'1 – 2 – 3 CLICK!'

(Wait 5 secs at most then say...)

'You can remember your name again.'

(If you acted like you reached over and took the name out reach back and put it in as you say the above.)

Hands totally stick alternative script.

'Ok clasp your hands together like this... (palms together; fingers interlaced as if praying desperately)

...Now, have you ever had **your hands stick to something** *and you couldn't get*

it off? Have you ever stuck your hands with superglue? Maybe it was embarrassing I don't know? Maybe **you got stuck** *in really sticky mud like I did on a camping trip?* **It was so sticky** *it sucked our wellies (wellington boots) off. Or maybe when you were making dough as a child? All that incredibly sticky stuff on your fingers!* (Think of universal experiences.)

Now **imagine** *I have some incredibly super powerful super-glue; and what do you imagine it would feel like as I* **squeeze** *that glue into those gaps between your fingers and hands* **sticking them all together, now.** *You can* **feel that** *superglue between those/your hands hardening sticking together. I want you to* **feel it instantly hardening and getting stickier and stickier with every passing second, now.**

In a few seconds I'll count from 1-3 and say **stuck!** *And* **those hands will be stuck solid** *and no matter how hard you*

try **they remain stuck!** *In a moment*
verify they won't move *to your own*
satisfaction.

1-2-3 **STUCK!'**

Let them struggle for 3-5 seconds only then
say...

'Release!'

**Note - if doing waking hypnosis and not
eyes shut hypnosis:** *at each moment, each
stage in the 5 step process look for the* **'it's
sunk in'** *look. Glassy eyes, skin tonus
alteration etc. Be patient and wait for it – do
not progress till you get it.*

As the victim/Jedi slave does what you ask at
each stage of these processes you can
condition them by saying,

'Good,' then move on. If you like.

Your get out of jail card.

If it fails, and now and again it will, say
something like,

'Great you're **that** *kind of person, I suspected*

it, now that really helps me help you and we'll do something else.'

<u>*Hallucinations are best achieved by...*</u>

Just be direct: say,

'When you open your eyes you will/will not see x.'

X being whatever positive or negative hallucination you want them to have.

Positive hallucination = '...you see a shark floating around the room (plus safety feature) but it doesn't scare you.'

This was the gag/routine I most remember from hypno-dog man.

Negative hallucination = '...when you open your eyes you can't see any pens. They all just vanished etc.!'

The great hypnotist Milton Erickson was doing a talk on hypnosis and asked for volunteers. Some people came on stage and he simply shouted without warning and pointed at the side stage wall,

'What colour is that dog!!!'

And the volunteers instantly 'tranced out' and saw a 'dog.' He was that good.

No matter what happens: always remain calm and enjoy yourself. After all what's the bl**dy point otherwise????! People are different. Go out and FAIL it will teach you much! When it does fail and it will occasionally, remember – you'll live, no one died. It's no big deal. When you don't fear failure and know it can happen –you'll paradoxically relax.

Remember: when you want to do a 'hypno-gimmick' frame it by

- *Activating their imagination and...*

- *Comparing it to something they've done, perhaps in another context.*

The hypnotic principles of: **memory** (what has been), **imagination** (what could be), **re-association** (activating resources).

Analyse this!

In closing: your powerful critical mind is your self-defence against unwanted influence. Use it, analyse, **think, think think!** Is this true? How do I know it's true? Check the sources: ***assume nothing.***

Epilogue: the creepy future of 'hypnosis': electronic thought installation????!

The following came from:

Advertising Age

'Hear Voices? It May Be an Ad'

An A&E Billboard 'Whispers' a Spooky Message Audible Only in Your Head in Push to Promote Its New 'Paranormal' Program.

By Andrew Hampp Published: December 10, 2007.

In New York people heard a woman's voice right in their mind asking,

'Who's there? Who's there?'

People looked about; no one there!

Then the voice said, 'It's not your imagination.'

It was an advert for 'Paranormal State,' a ghost-themed series premiering on A and E (a US TV network for Brits and Europeans). The new billboard technology was created by

'Holosonic' and transmitted from an 'audio spotlight' from a rooftop speaker so that the sound was projected: **within people's heads.** The company responsible claimed it was a '...less-intrusive approach.' (??????!) 'The whole idea is to spare other people,' a spokesman said.

Inducing 'schizophrenia' as a new ad gimmick. Hmmm? Isn't your headspace inviolate? Does anyone have the right to violate it because it suits them???! Do you want messages beamed into your head against your will!?

The spokesman, a certain Mr. Pompei (the place destroyed by a cataclysmic event?!) said further that some people might complain at first but '...they'll see it's effective for **getting attention**.'

I'm quite sure that it is.

On that rather chilling note I shall leave you young Padawan! Use your knowledge to make people feel good and remember if you hear 'funny' voices in your head-space: it's just 'progress.'

I hope you enjoyed your read.

COMING SOON! 'WIZARDS OF TRANCE!'

- Book 5 in the series will give you the hypnotic persuasion strategies and more of the best, greatest and not so well known 'hypnotists,' propagandists, influence masters and public relations experts down through time – this stuff goes way back!!!

- These are the people I call – 'The Wizards of trance!' It will give in depth knowledge as to how crowds (the human herd) have been 'nudged' and hypnotised throughout history! Plus...erm, some other stuff like the language of fake psychics with *a full transcript of a genuine spooky tarot card session exposed.* We will also examine the masterful hypnosis and hypnotherapy techniques of the most important hypnotherapists of the 20th century: the ones who invented **_effective_** modern hypnosis. You might not have heard of all of them!

- I thought I'd have room to cover more topics in this book, I apologise, I didn't – this will end up an encyclopaedia otherwise. I'll cover advanced political 'hopenosis' in the next one too and more! *Watch this space baby!* 'Hypnosis' is a much wider topic than you know!

Goodbye for now,

R.H signing off.

Your appendixeseses...I mean your appendiceses...oh some scripts and other helpful gibberish have been tagged on at the end! See ya!

YOUR BONUSES: Extended appendix.

The appendix in this volume is somewhat different from the appendices in my other books; there is no repetition of the mass of scripts already provided for your learning and amusement, rather I have included a collection of bonus material and interesting topics not yet covered that should improve your growing hypnosis mastery. I have done this to show how much I appreciate your taking the time to buy and read my little bookie.

Appendix 1: analysis of old time stage hypnosis routine.

Imagine a reasonable sized theatre full of victims/volunteers for an old time stage hypnosis show; maybe the hypnotist is wearing a cape and turban? Who knows!? Often stage hypnotists will play motivational music from Star Wars (drawing on the 'force') or the theme from the Superman movies (you have super powers!). You could say 'Drum roll please!' But we're not going to use any of that: our 'weapons' are words.

(Remember before the show starts all the somnambulists and even those who unconsciously desire to be hypnotised are already primed, their minds have been getting ready since they bought the ticket! Especially if the hypnotist is very famous, our friends <u>prestige</u> and <u>expectation</u> are afoot!)

He begins...

'Ladies and gentleman I require complete silence...

(Here our man tells everyone to 'shut up'

- all voices, including the thinking voice - indirectly and so <u>focus</u> on him/<u>sensory deprivation</u> begins. The first blatant <u>compliance test</u> is given.)

In order to test for the best volunteers we will perform a hypnotic hand clasp. All of you join in please; only this way will we find the most talented hypnotic subjects! It is a test of relaxation and concentration.

(<u>Presupposition</u> – I want the best somnambulists not the riff raff; this primes the somnambulists to respond. A hand clasp was and is a standard test that many people have heard of or seen in a hypnotic show; <u>expectation</u> is utilised. When EVERYONE joins in, the suggestibility of the entire crowd is enhanced: the creation of the de-individualised '<u>group-mind.</u>' Frame set: indirect 'relax and concentrate' command given through <u>implication.</u>)

Look into my eyes! Extend your arms thus! (He demonstrates how – arms straight out and parallel) *And squeeze your hands together!*

(Hypnotic gaze expected by group – attention fixated, hypnotic process is beginning overtly; unconscious is being primed and pumped to prepare more. Compliance test 2 and plausible cultural ritual: extend arms and squeeze! 'Squeeze' also suggestive of things sticking together. All direct commands said authoritatively with the hypnotist's expectation that they will be followed, his voice evidences no doubt of success. His hypnotic intent is strong.)

You are now unable to separate your hands because they are locked together... (This is repeated once or twice.)

(A direct hypnotic command is given with a negative too – 'unable' – negatives work; only cults want constant 'positive' languaging. 'Because' - pseudo-plausible cause and effect. Repetition to drill in command and ensure subconscious knows clearly what is required and so can produce it on cue.)

The harder you try to pull your hands apart

the tighter they stick!

(Repeat and hold gaze firmly.)

(Law of reversed effort – 'try' if you try to do something you can't do it. 'The' - hypnotic conjunction for pseudo cause effect, compounding suggestions atop one another and feedback loop.)

On the count of 1-2-3 you will be unable to separate those hands!

(Repeat etc.)

(Subconscious is given *trigger* to create desired effect by. Not now but 'in a moment pattern' implied 'on the count' – *indirect command* – hands stick together.)

1-2-3! (Say with dramatic effect! Now check to see whose hands are stuck – these are your best subjects, soon you bring them up on stage.)

(Hypnotic phenomena trigger fired!)

On the count of 3 you will be unable to keep your eyes open at all and you will fall into a deep hypnotic sleep! (Look to see who continues to follow commands.)

(Hypnotist immediately makes further test to seek the best somnambulists. Old trigger reused because subconscious has accepted it – will work all the time now and streamlines things. Indirect command for eye closure and 'instant' deep hypnosis. Keep moving: give the conscious mind no time to kick in – overload the suckers and fast!)

Open your eyes on 3 but you will not awaken from hypnotic sleep!'

(Trigger set up. Word 'but' implies reversal, see book 2, 'Mastering hypnotic language.' Zombie waking hypnosis 'asked for.')

Close your eyes and fall even deeper into hypnotic sleep than before! (Check for compliance – weed out the 'disobedient.')

(<u>Fractionation</u> – open and close eyes etc. <u>Deepener</u> command's given.)

Go deeper and deeper into deep hypnotic

sleep!

(Direct deepening, semi-repetitious/boring/mantra like — narrowing focus. Notice although he framed 'relaxation' at the beginning our man has not said relax once!)

In a moment I'll count from 1-3 and on 3 it will be impossible for you to open your eyes no matter how forcefully you try!'

(Finally — last test given; eye catalepsy. <u>Apposition of opposites:</u> any force used aids the closure!)

Your slaves are cooked, now you play. The same principles recycled over and over in varying guises. Getting the idea?

Appendix 2: Pleasure symbol waking hypnosis convincer script.

Create waking hypnosis then use this symbology pleasure convincer. Don't pinch someone's arm to test for analgesia, get their arm to lift etc. - that's what every other unoriginal twit does; **people like any excuse to feel pleasure**, as I have said in my other books - they never resist. You can use it in 'normal' eyes closed hypnosis too.

(This is powerful; use only with a sense of responsibility please!)

Pleasure symbology script.

(Deep hypnosis assumed)

'Just for fun

imagine...

let come to mind...

in its own time...

a symbol that represents

your own personal feelings of intense pleasure/joy etc.

The most powerful...

amazing...

life-affirming...

natural state of **pleasure** you can feel.

(Give them time to get one.)

Accept the subconscious symbol given without question.

Now, that symbol represents feelings...

your feelings of intense pleasure (etc.)

put that symbol in that part of your body

where it deeply desires to go...

because pleasure...

like all feelings...

has a natural home somewhere inside...

let that symbol move there.

(Pause to let it happen...)

Great.

Now let these powerful feelings of intense pleasure

spread out from that place...

That's it!

Let them build and build and only intensify!

More and more and more...

Better and better, even better!

Let them radiate all through you

getting stronger and stronger

feeling that amazing pleasure only grow

and build...

feeling incredible...

you **feel that pleasure so intensely.**

It's almost as though

you want to **bathe in these feelings**

for a while...

luxuriate in them...

go on...

you deserve this...

As they continue to grow

and actually become so intense

that

**these amazingly powerful feelings
of pleasure spread**

out beyond your body!

They are that powerful.

Let your feeling of wonderful, blissful pleasure

build to a wonderful

pleasurable peak of pleasure!

That's it!

And as a gift...

keep just the right level

of that feeling of deep

profound pleasure with you

and find that

you have more pleasure naturally

in waking life, now.'

Appendix 3: The structure of hypnotically eliciting waking 'feeling states' in anyone.

The formula for eliciting feelings in the waking state is easy; let's keep it simple and use relaxation...

1. What is distinct about the desired state? What makes it x and not y?

'Relaxation is a state of peace of mind and body. The absence to a greater or lesser degree of mental and physical tension. The sympathetic phase of the nervous system is taking over – you calm down after any arousal.'

You have now set the frame and direction of awareness.

2. How does the desired process actually occur?

'Relaxation can occur in many ways. You can be absorbed in something. You can focus on your muscles relaxing. You can daydream. You can lie down and take it easy. You can remember or imagine something relaxing etc.'

You can give examples: 'when you're in nature,' 'lazing on the sofa,' etc.

3. How does this process intensify?

'Relaxation can develop by continuing with any of the processes mentioned for a prolonged period of time. It can also intensify with more and more absorption in these processes to the exclusion of anything else.'

See it's easy: to _understand_ this - people will have to _experience_ it – especially women. They will use feelings first and then logic to understand this type of talk. Tips for eliciting states conversationally are: really think – what is this state and what isn't it? Think what its opposite is. Keep it vague when describing it. There are other ways to elicit states conversationally but I'll leave those for another time.

Appendix 4: Pretending to be hypnotised script, advanced Ericksonian hypnosis and more.

Here's some Ericksonian influenced approaches you could use with clients. You might not need to use embeds; I put them in to weigh things in your favour. Erickson found that when people tried to prove him a fraud by pretending to be hypnotised, real hypnosis developed??!

Pretend to be hypnotised induction.

(You could ask someone to close their eyes or keep them open)

'You ever heard the saying, 'fake it till you make it,'? (Idea seeding/priming.)

Ok, you have, great, do you know

that over 90 years of research into hypnosis

has proven that if you just

fake **going into hypnosis...**

you can **really enter it, now.**

In fact like a method actor...

you could fake the whole thing so well...

that **real hypnosis develops...**

All you have to do is **simulate hypnosis realistically...**

How would a hypnotised person behave?

How would they sit?

How would their **breathing alter?**

How little tension would that body need?

Just pretend...

as you did **as a child...** (pleasant age regression)

when you played but really believed

in those imaginary realities your own imagination conjured...

and as you **allow yourself** to pretend

I don't know what kind of **trance** will develop, (presupposition that trance WILL occur)

that will be for you to discover, **now.**

In hypnosis

muscle tone can change... (describing trance can elicit it)

the eye moves or doesn't in a different way...

nothing bothers one...

people respond or don't in ways differing from wakefulness...

perceptions alter for a while...

and won't it be interesting...

aren't you curious just how and when such things will manifest?

Thaaa-at's it.'

Troubleshooting Ericksonain style.

Someone says to you,

'I dare you to hypnotise me!'   (The more angry, affronted they are the better!)

Look them in the eye and say,

'Oh, I <u>wouldn't</u> dare. **That's what you'll have to do all by yourself.'**

(Now completely ignore them – they may well spontaneously develop trance.)

Someone says,

'I really want to experience hypnosis!'

Say in an offhand way, as though it has no importance,

'If wishes were horses beggars might ride.'

(They may well go into instant trance.)

<u>*Ways to seed trance.*</u>

'Would you like to **experience trance?'**

'Have you ever been in communion with **your/re** *own thoughts –* **deeply engrossed** *in them?'*

'Perhaps it rained all day and you thought, 'I'll have to **go inside?'**

'Can you discover the processes in thinking

through from beginning to end, any specified task?'

Ask while they are hypnotised,

'Where are you...OR aren't you?'

The following questions etc. can be used to seed trance or deepen it. If the subject is already hypnotised or not, just before you ask such questions say, *'This is private - you don't need to answer, just be aware of that response.'* You needn't use all the questions.

'Do you think you can be hypnotised?'

'Will you know when you are hypnotised?'

'Are you hypnotised right now?'

'Are you in trance?'

'Are you not hypnotised?'

'Is your behaviour that of someone who is not hypnotised?'

'What don't you understand about this?'

'How do you feel about this?'

'Are you satisfied that you are hypnotised?'

'You are relaxed; what does this mean?'

'In trance you can be responsive and aware of the immediate past and current present.'

'What is not understood?'

'Does x make sense?'

'Review your responses and consider them...'

Early in his career Erickson described hypnosis as **'non-waking awareness'**; what do you think?

Appendix 5: A very short 'Geometric Progression' script for permanency of change.

So-called hypnotic 'geometric progression' which was developed by Milton Erickson can be used in a number of contexts. What is it? What does it do? You can prepare the subconscious for permanent change of habits by letting it get the idea that all it has to do is extend the altered behaviour one second more at a time and then one second more and then two seconds, two minutes, two hours etc. Thereby the change doesn't seem so dramatic although it is – it is a type of reframe. I use it sometimes with drug addicts who have trouble staying 'clean,' of course I do a lot more than that, but it's a part of the whole caboodle.

Geometric progression.

'If someone stops doing something for months on end, then one second more is nothing, neither is one minute, half an hour, an hour, two hours, ten hours, half the day, you sleep at night so you already know how to stop and do other things, one day, one month, two

months, six months and one second, one year and one second, two years and on and on and on...small incremental changes lead to lasting results, now...'

Short and sweet and to the point, no need to waffle.

Appendix 6: He bweathed me to sweep! Using tone alone and breathing rates to induce trance and altered states.

'There is an awake rate of breathing...

There is a sleeping rate of breathing...

There is an entranced rate of breathing...

There is an hypnotic rate of breathing...

There are rates of breathing associated will all emotional states...

Our breathing changes as we concentrate...

As we fall asleep...

As anyone enters trance, now...

There is a deeply relaxed and restful rate of breathing...

Calmness manifests and feeds-back on a particular breathing rate.

When your tone gradually calms...

is smoother...

more knowingly rhythmical,

hypnotically rhythmical...

and you just know that rhythm instinctively...

and when you slow...your...voice...down...

and speak with more meaning and purpose...

people's unconscious minds see this as a cue to enter trance...

it is......an......unspoken cue......to slow......things......down......

more....and.....more......

and.........go.........inside...

Milton Erickson...used to use this...with children in hospitals who wouldn't sleep...

He would match their breathing rate...pacing their...ongoing experience...

And then he'd slow his down...to the rate of a sleeping person...

he did this to a little boy...and children notice things...that adults don't...

because no one told them yet not to notice...and the little boy said...

'He bweethed me to sweep.'

Just as when you think...more slowly...

and calm down your inner voice...you feel so much more relaxed...

Some hypnotist's advise giving suggestions on a client's outbreath...

because when someone breathes out...they relax more...

and so become more suggestible...use this information...

as you see best...in being the best hypnotist you can be, really be,

knowing at a deep level that *you can hypnotise anyone*...

Noooooooooo-ooooooooow.'

Appendix 7: How to construct your own 'early learning set.'

Erickson created a form of age regression he called 'the early learning set.' Its purpose was to revivify a time in the patient/client's life when they were in a 'learning' frame of mind. Obviously the time when we are intensely learning about reality etc. is when we are/were young children, perhaps in the context of formal education within the state mandated compulsory education system. ***Avoid any mention of early childhood if you suspect abuse memories that may be accessed.***

I use the following script as a deepener from time to time: it follows the principle of 'state dependent learning,' the idea that there is an optimum and personal learning state that we all have, it may differ from person to person but it's there. Studies have shown that when you learn in that state and are tested/perform in that same state you are much more likely to recall/retrieve the necessary info.

<u>NOTE FOR THE TERMINALLY STUPID:</u>
<u>HYPNOTIC LANGUAGE IS SUPPOSED TO</u>
<u>BE GRAMMATICALLY INCORRECT! THIS</u>
<u>IS WHAT MAKES IT HYPNOTIC!!!</u>

<u>Early learning set.</u>

'And now, as you continue there and hear
listening

at some level to what I'm saying

the things that will assist you to –

deepen that relaxed trance
comfortably

and you can in any way that you want

ponder several appropriate things.

One of which can really mesmerize you

and **remembering** like you did as a child...

a favourite teacher,

maybe a story...or storyteller,

those learning experiences maybe 6 or 7,

certainly at an age back then with those little chairs,

the numbers and letters around the room,

up on the wall and already –

you're altering –

and your curious unconscious mind can really learn

learning the difference between a big O and a big Q

and whether 6 was an upside 9 or 9 was an upside down 6

and you learned how to turn those letters into words,

thoughts,

ideas,

complete ideas,

deeper and deeper ideas,

ideas that occupy all of you

as it **time stands still or slows right**

down

for a while because...

you don't have to do anything else

and anyone could ask of yourself

is the body on this chair, pressing down
comfortably

or is the chair pressing up
against...supporting.

Ever so gently yet securely...

as you continue to orient your mind

to **begin to ponder, really ponder**

about what you want to **change now**...

you might start to

create the change you want and it can be secret change.

There was a time even further back

where you had the potential to learn to talk,

a time before these sounds became

meaningful.

Humans have many potentials, and you can, can you not?

How soon will your trance deepen further?

And you can

follow your own associative processes to these words,

can you not? Meaningful symbols.

And can you follow the symbolic meanings,

associations of the word **comfort** and follow where it leads you.

On occasion it can be very good and pleasant enjoying

letting go of certain directions and controls

to permit unconscious autonomous processes to take over, now...

In the course of living from infancy on you acquired knowledge but you could not keep that knowledge in the foreground of your mind.

And there is no need to talk if you haven't already...'

Appendix 8: The RH's variant of the Ericksonian 'handshake' induction.

This is a pattern interrupt. It can be as simple as this...

- Set hypnotic context.

- Say, 'I didn't catch your name?'

- When they tell you their name go to shake their hand.

- As though it's all quite normal gently grab their wrist instead and turn their palm toward them. **(They will go into instant confusion! NOT NORMAL – it will stun them!)**

- Lift their hand toward their face and hold it before their eyes. **(Fixate attention.)**

- Say, 'Look at all the details of **a** hand. Notice the lines, the varying colours you never noticed. Look at the wrinkles and bumps – **become absorbed** by **that** hand. *A part of you yet a part*

of you.' **('a' and 'that' –
dissociative.)**

- Gently move their hand closer and closer to their face. **(Non-verbal intensification of focus/look out for trance signals – see book 1.)**

- Say, 'When you hand touches your face, close your eyes and **SLEEP!**' **(In a moment pattern: see book 2, 'Mastering hypnotic language.')**

- Push their hand over their eyes **(Non-verbal suggestion)**. Check for eye closure. If you have it say...

- 'Good. Let this hand fall and as it falls you can **go all the way down, now.'** **(Dropping hand is a non-verbal for going <u>down, falling into hypnosis.)</u>**

- Let it drop.

- Say, 'That's right!'

- Proceed to _capture imagination_ with deepeners.

<u>Troubleshooting – if they are sitting or
standing get ready to catch them!</u>

In 'Wizards of trance' I will show you the best
instant inductions I know of!

NOTE AND WARNING: You are responsible for others' safety while they are hypnotised. Think of them as young children with NO sense of danger.

Appendix 9: A new hypnotic induction script – intensifying trance without saying the word relax!

This is a high intensity focus script without the use of the word relax – this will render the experience primarily a mental rather than a physical affair, some hypnotists (and I am not one of them) believe only mental hypnosis is needed; I include it here as an option.

High intensity focus induction script.

'Please just close your eyes...

and in your mind's eye...

focus on your left hand knuckle of your forefinger...

notice it...

any sensations

you notice there...

fixate your attention on that one place...now.

How would you feel if you had to

focus intently on something that was

really important?

Maybe like you're life depended on that, so

you're focusing intensely like that, now...

Many things can attract our attention,

sometimes just one thing, now...

Did you ever **concentrate on something** so much...

that you **forget about anything else** for a while?

Athletes experience that when **you go into the zone...**

Great actors do it when **you give something your full attention...**

Think of the word **focus!**

There are many times when we

become deeply absorbed in an activity...

it becomes the sole **focus** of our attention...

perhaps one time like that can come to mind?

We can **become intensely fascinated** by our daydreams, can't you?

Everyone has experienced that...

As a child you did it often...

and you can **experience a captivating and relevant daydream now.**

(We deepen hypnosis by intensifying it – some hypnotists call deepeners 'intensifiers' I agree with this, we are just intensifying the state of focus...)

In a moment, not right this instant but very soon...

I will say the name of a relevant letter

That will allow the deepest part of you to

intensify this pleasant state...

this can happen as soon as I say...'now!'

I want you to see the letter F in your mind...

Now...

see that F

F for **focus intently...**

see its shape...

The font...

The style...

The colour of that F

for **FOCUS intently...**

Fantastic...

Ok, in a few seconds I'll say the name of another letter

And when I do you can

intensify this state even more...

See a letter O in your mind, now!

O for **only this state of mind...**

Notice all its qualities...

as **this absorbing state only**

increases...

On the next letter you can focus even more on what is of sole/soul importance...

a place of **no distractions...**

See that C now!

C for **concentrate your attention** intensely, inside...

What is it about that concentrating letter that grabs your attention so?

Next letter only allows you to **intensify this state...**

in your own unique way...

to the exclusion of everything else...

U/You, now!

See that U...

which can stand for that uplifting feeling we get when

you're intensely in flow...

that state of mind where everything just seems to go right...

almost magically so...

when you just trust the subconscious to take over...

and you almost watch yourself

doing what you need to effortlessly...

Notice the exact qualities of that U

that only intensify this state a little more.

One last time for luck...

feeling good

about your own innate ability to **be captivated by something...**

Can you guess the last letter?

The one that will...

intensify this state just as much as is needed...

to **concentrate your mind** on getting

precisely what it is that you want.

See that S now!

That S for your success in this session...

Perhaps you can consider at a very deep level

precisely the success you deeply desire...

as certain unconscious patterns shift to allow this to happen naturally...

You just spelt the word **FOCUS!**

So can you get a clear image of what kind of changes you want...

and **intensely focus on those pleasing possibilities, now?**

That's right.'

Appendix 10: Stopping an allergic reaction using authoritarian hypnosis.

Hypnosis scripts don't have to be long, they can be very short and work spectacularly. For self-hypnosis you might want to keep them short and sweet at first – into hypnosis quick, quick intervention – out fast. Some therapists do this and it works a treat. <u>You don't go all permissive in an emergency!</u> If someone needs quick help and they are in danger they are highly suggestible – whack them under fast and say this in a commanding, no nonsense tone...

<u>Short stop allergic reaction script.</u>

(Hypnosis, hypnoidal or suggestible state assumed)

'Ok subconscious you are in charge of this person.

you have allowed a particular reaction to occur...

Thank you...

but there is no genuine toxin...

X (banana/s etc.) is not toxic…

I know you intend this reaction to protect this person…

it is a well-intentioned, but unpleasant,

unnecessary and potentially dangerous reaction,

it is counter-productive to your genuine desire…

STOP IT NOW!

Let their physiological reactions return to normal

as quickly, as safely as you possibly can

because that is what is now best for this person

at this time in their life…

calm that reaction down, now…

What's best for this person in all ways…

is to **return to normal functioning now…**

You know that's what's best...

there is no real problem...

you are safe...

this person is safe...

they can and should be allowed to...

feel well again...

You created this reaction but this reaction is not needed

so you can **change this reaction, now.'**

Carry on in this vein until the person's symptoms subside. Embeds aren't needed BUT they load things your way. The negotiation protocol for effective authoritarian hypnosis is:

- Accept and acknowledge the subconscious has good intentions. Thank it.

- Say that x (symptom/problem) is counterproductive and list reasons.

- Offer immediate re-direction of how the subconscious should behave. TELL IT!

- Remember the subconscious is running the show.

- **NOTE AND WARNING: DO NOT USE HYPNOSIS ORDINARILY IN THE EVENT OF ACTUAL POISONING AS DOCTORS WILL USE SYMPTOMS TO FIND THE CURE! EVEN IF AN ALLERGIC REACTION IS SUSPECTED SEEK MEDICAL ADVICE INSTANTLY: HYPNOSIS IS NOT A REPLACEMENT FOR SUITABLE MEDICAL ATTENTION. THIS SCRIPT IS PROVIDED FOR IN EXTREMIS CIRCUMSTANCES!!! THIS IS LIFE OR DEATH STUFF!**

The secrets of self-hypnosis will be covered in a future book devoted solely to this popular topic. Watch this space in 2014. I will provide full, original scripts: the lot!

Appendix 11: The classic blackboard deepener; RH's version of it.

Many things associated with school, learning etc. are hypnotic. School is a symbol of learning, of being moulded and shaped to fit into society as a 'well adjusted' member: i.e. 'an obedient worker ant.' Be that as it may here is the 'classic' blackboard deepener that we hypnotists often use, with my own twists added.

RH's classic 'Blackboard Deepener.'

'I want you to **imagine** yourself now –

standing in front of a blackboard...

you have a piece of coloured chalk in one hand...

and a cloth/eraser etc. in the other.

The blackboard is quite clean and clear...

empty of content...

but what I would like you to do –

is to take the chalk and draw on the blackboard the number 10.

(Pause a mo'.)

Lovely, now,

when you've done that you can just take that cloth/eraser and rub it out

so that the blackboard is clear once more.

And when that's done to your satisfaction

can you to take the piece of chalk...

and in the top right hand corner of the blackboard

simply write the word **sleep!**

The very hypnotic word **sleep!**

Clearly note the s and the l and the two e's and the p.

Sleep!

Notice the size of the word...

and the formation of the letters...

the exact position of the word **sleep** on the board...

And now, that you can see the word **sleep -**

and only when you can see the word **sleep -**

just use your cloth/eraser and wipe it all away

just wipe away the word – **sleep!**

And as you erase the word **sleep** from your mind –

you **find yourself becoming sleepier**

and much more comfortable and much more deeply relaxed.

That's right...

Now when that blackboard is clear...

and only when the blackboard is clear...

Use the coloured chalk and write the number 9!

(Pause a mo'.)

And when you can see the number 9 vividly...

and only when you can see the number 9

simply use that device to rub it out completely...

so that the blackboard is clear once more.

And when the blackboard is clear take that chalk

and in the top right hand corner of the blackboard...

as you have before...

write the word **sleep - sleep -**

the incredibly hypnotic word **sleep!**

Get a sense of seeing the s and the l and the two e's and the p.

What does it spell?

Sleep - notice the precise size of the word...

and the unique way you have formed the letters...

note the position of the word **sleep** on the board/bored...

and when you can see the word **sleep** –

and only when you can see the word **sleep!**

Simply use that cloth/eraser and wipe it all...away

wipe away that hypnotic word - **sleep -**

and as you remove the word sleep from your mind –

you **find yourself becoming so much sleepier**

and much more wondrously comfortable

and so much more profoundly relaxed, inside.

Now when the board is clear once more

and only when the blackboard is clear...

could you take your piece of chalk and write the number 8...

on the blackboard - and when you can see the number 8...

and only when you can see the number 8

just take the cloth/eraser and rub it out totally!

Rub out the number 8...

so that blackboard is free and empty for use.

Free for things of importance to be placed there...

to be imprinted deeply upon it.

(Pause a mo')

Fantastic! And I want you to continue in this manner

first of all drawing the number 7...

then wiping it all...away...

and then when the board is clear –

and only when the blackboard is clear –

you can write upon it the word **sleep**!

And as before so onward...

So with each succeeding number down to 0...

each time you wipe away the number or word

sleep –

you find yourself **drifting deeper and deeper**

into a **warm** and **sleepy** sort of **feeling...**

a **very relaxed** and a **very comfortable** sort of **feeling**

going deeper and deeper into hypnotic levels of relaxation...

And you might not even want to complete this task...

at some point, unconsciously, you might **just drift off...**

So just begin now...

carry out that hypnotising task...

with the number 7!

And as you do this...

I'm going to be talking directly to your subconscious mind,

of course the conscious mind is free to listen but need not...

It can just **remain comfortable and pleasantly rested** for while...

but you don't even need to **listen to me...**

because your subconscious mind will hear everything that it needs to hear.

For I am now talking to YOU the subconscious mind...

the dreaming mind...

ready and receptive to hypnotic learning...

and **deep profound change, now...**

And when you reach 0

you'll find yourself deeply hypnotised,

noooooooow...'

Penultimately - Appendix 12: Quick troubleshooting tips.

Hypnosis need not be complex, it can be very simple and yet still effective, here are a few pointers and tricks to assist you. The first 2 are quick deepeners.

Counting backwards.

'Soon I want you to simply count backwards

from 500...

and as you **focus on that task...**

gradually

at some point...

you'll **drift off...**

your **mind** could **wander...**

perhaps

that inner voice becomes slower...

or you just stop counting down at some point

and **go deeper into hypnosis, now.'**

Remember the keys of your PC: The Qwertyuiop deepener.

'Just visualise the keys of a keyboard...

maybe on an old fashioned typewriter...

maybe on a kindle, a nook, a touch screen of some type...

maybe on your PC...

Now the first line spells – QWERTYUIOP! (QWERTIOOIOP!)

Visualise each key individually...

see it clearly in your mind's eye...

just as it appears on that keyboard...

and **each letter only takes you deeper...**

Q

W

E

R

T

Y

U

I

O

P

Perfect!

Now the next line...which spells – ASDFGHJKL! (ASDAFICAJICAL!)

As you see each letter **you go deeper...**

See the...

A

S

D

F

G

H

J

K

L

Lovely...

And finally just see the last line...

and that allows you to **go much deeper into hypnosis...**

than you already were, with each letter...

that you see...ZXCVBNM (ZUKVUBNUM!)

Z

X

C

V

B

N

M...

Marvellous...

deeply hypnotised...

realising...

you're entranced

as we **pleasantly** continue...now...'

<u>No:21 re-induction.</u>

(This is used to set up a post hypnotic command trigger near a session's end)

'Whenever I say the number 21...

or anything associated with that number...

that adds up to that number...

that when subtracted equals that number...

or anything else I might devise...

for example

I might say,

'What are 3 7s?'

And **when that occurs**

you will instantly enter a state of

deep hypnotic sleep...

(Options...)

and close your eyes/even if your eyes are wide open...

and go 50 times deeper than this one.

That's right.'

Finally - Appendix 13 (lucky for some??): Short self-esteem boost story time...

13! Unlucky for some: lucky for you. Precisely targeted change work need not be long and drawn out. Dr. Erickson once said something like this to a client,

'Your subconscious mind can raise your self-worth for its own unconscious reasons.'

I have done this with clients: it works. Hypnotic stories are covered extensively in book 3, 'Powerful hypnosis,' they are powerful change-work tools. Let me leave you with this charming apocryphal tale because...

<u>Michelangelo's angel script.</u>

'...That reminds me of a story...

The following short tale is said to be about a great artist;

unproven but credited to him.

One swelteringly hot summer's day in Florence...

a little Italian boy saw an intense, young man chipping away at a large piece of rock.

'Why are you doing that?' he asked the man.

'Because,' said Michelangelo, wiping the sweat from his brow,

'There is an angel inside, and s/he wants to come out.'

Now that's one big bargain bucket book if I may say so myself!

Printed in Great Britain
by Amazon

41498073R00347